Christian Unity: Matrix for Mission

Paul A. Crow, Jr.

Friendship Press   **New York**

BX
8.2
.C7
1982

Library of Congress Cataloging in Publication Data

Crow, Paul A.
  Christian unity.

  Includes bibliographical references.
  1. Ecumenical movement.   2. Church—Unity.   I. Title
  BX8.2.C7   270.8'2   81-15285
  ISBN 0-377-00115-5   AACR2

ISBN: 0-377-00115-5
Editorial Office: 475 Riverside Drive, Room 772, New York, NY 10115
Distribution Office: PO Box 37844, Cincinnati, OH 45237

Copyright © 1982 by Friendship Press, Inc.
Printed in the United States of America

Contents

For my father, **Paul A. Crow**
whose life has been a hymn of peace and reconciliation
and who taught unity as a family adventure, and

for my mother, **Beulah Parker Crow**
who spent her seventy years of servanthood as a living
witness to the unity of the Church, and who understood
that unity comes through the Cross.

"Remember that through your parents you were born;
and what can you give back to them that equals their
gift to you?" (Ecclesiasticus 7:28)

PREFACE

Jeremiah Burroughes, a seventeenth-century ecumenist, gave his *Irenicum* (their word for a book about Christian unity) a delightful subtitle: *To the Lovers of Truth and Peace; Heart-Divisions opened in the causes of Evil, with cautions that we may not be hurt by them, and Endeavors to heal them.* Fortunately ecumenical books now carry shorter titles, but they still necessarily make comprehensive claims, calling the readers to wider loyalties in the faith.

This book is a primer, a book of first principles about Christian unity and the ecumenical calling in today's world. It is not a world survey of all ecumenical developments or a practical handbook for every ecumenical problem. I am convinced that neither of those resources will be helpful until a more fundamental task has been done, namely engaging, teaching and converting a new generation of Christians to their baptismal call to the unity of the people of God. This book, therefore, is a testament and deliberately holds up the vision of Christian unity in a radically changing world situation. It interprets Christian unity as an essential part of the gospel and a responsibility of all Christians. Grasping this vision involves discovering what it means to believe that God has *already* made us one in Christ and to make those decisions that will draw the whole people of God into a vibrant, witnessing community.

Writing a book always reminds us of those who have influenced us and those to whom we owe special debts. The production of this book was particularly enhanced by Michael K. Kinnamon, a worthy partner in dialogue, who serves on the Faith and Order secretariat of the World Council of Churches; and to two helpmates at the Ecumenical Institute Bossey outside Geneva, Corrien Jansen, a Bossey Blue Angel from Holland who cheerfully typed the various drafts, and Barbara Hertz, whose skills in language proved very helpful.

CHRISTIAN UNITY: MATRIX FOR MISSION

W.A. Visser 't Hooft, Karl Hertz, Robert Welsh and David Taylor read the full manuscript and gave wise counsel. Others who played notably helpful diaconal roles are Jerry Boney, Gwen Cashmore, Stephen P. Crow, Carol Crow Phillips, Rosemary Green, Dan Martensen, Gerald F. Moede, J. Robert Nelson, Sister Pierrette of Grandchamp, Thomas Ryan, David Thompson, Max Thurian of Taizé and Thomas Wieser. My thanks also go to Margaret Koch, librarian of the Ecumenical Institute Bossey; Ans van der Bent, librarian of the World Council of Churches; Ward L. Kaiser, executive director of Friendship Press, who warmly supported the project at every stage; and to those members of the Commission on Education for Mission of the National Council of the Churches of Christ in the U.S.A. who saw the significance of this theme for the churches.

More than I can adequately say in these brief words, the birth and maturation of this book was sustained in very special ways by the Board of Directors of the Council on Christian Unity of the Christian Church (Disciples of Christ) who understand the value of a study leave for the renewal of the church's leadership and gave a preoccupied president six months of spiritual creativity; by my staff at the Council on Christian Unity — Robert Welsh, Nita Floe Hempfling and Josi Beeler—who calmly bore additional burdens in the Disciples ecumenical office during my absence; and finally by my wife Mary and our daughter Susan, who shared these marvelous months at Bossey and sensed the importance of this book for the man who worked in the Salon de Genève.

Paul A. Crow, Jr.

The Ecumenical Institute Bossey, Switzerland
Pentecost, 1981

1 Unity, Diversity and Division

Never resign yourself to the scandal of the division of Christians.
—**The Rule of Taizé**

From my childhood in a small Alabama town I remember our Disciples congregation frequently singing the ecumenical faith:

We are not divided;
All one body we:
One in hope and doctrine,
One in charity.

I can remember till this day the spiritual fervor and conviction in those saintly voices. From time to time the minister would preach about Christian unity, and mandate us directly from the New Testament church or from our "historic plea." Only as I began to experience the church beyond those lyrics did I discover in Lanett, Alabama, and later elsewhere, the deep contradiction between the proclamation of unity in Christ on the one hand and the lack of understanding and living relations among Christians on the other. Two of my close friends were a Southern Baptist and a Roman Catholic, and at strategic times in my life both the pastor and the priest sent signals of alienation ("you don't belong") to me and my church.

The Methodists were only a block away from the First Christian Church on the square, but beyond their Wesleyan piety they were rumored to be the church to join if you had executive ambitions in the local textile mill. The Congregational Christian Church was appreciated by the others primarily for its gospel singing. The Pentecostals, unkindly called "the Holy Rollers," were located in the poor white part of the town. The black churches—Baptist and Christian Methodist Episcopal — worshiped and served to God's glory but were in many instances isolated in the ghetto section. Neither the Episcopal nor the Church of Christ nor the Primitive Baptist nor the Nazarene congregations had any real communication with the other churches in Lanett; each singularly called the saved and the unsaved to their own more excellent way. Twelve churches competed for the souls of that community in divided, blissful isolation. The atmosphere was rarely uncharitable; the community was characterized by cordial polemics and polite fragmentation, in the manner of a couple who had divorced but decided still to be friends. The churches' given unity in Christ was an unrealized hope. In countless places throughout the *oikoumene* (God's whole world), a similar portrait of the church can be painted. Unity is confessed, but division is accepted as normal and diversity is misunderstood. It is a classic case of a fundamental ecumenical problem: how does this pattern of unity, diversity and division fit into God's plan for people?

JOYOUS DIVERSITY AND UNHAPPY DIVISIONS

Just as unity is a gift of God, so also is diversity. Variety is God's gracious purpose for the human family. In the colorful array of creation, individuals reveal divine creativity through different cultures, languages, nations, races, art, personalities, persuasion and food. All are hues in the spectrum we call the people of God. All testify to the same Creator God. Furthermore, Christians witness to legitimate diversity in their faithfulness to Jesus Christ. The church, God's redeemed order, is characterized by differing sizes and shapes, a diversity of belief, worship, spirituality and structures all inspired by one and the same Spirit who apportions gifts to each one individually (1 Cor. 12:11). The New Testament witnesses to an astonishing diversity of theology and forms, yet with a vision of unity. Neither the diversity of creation nor the diversity in the Christian community are at odds with unity. The differences found in creation are not exclusive, but are complementary and mutually enriching realities manifesting the unity that God intended for creation. Similarly, the diversity of gifts in the church is an expression of the unity of all the members of the community.[1] The ecumenical movement has consistently affirmed that unity in diversity is its goal, notwithstanding the caricatures of those opponents who see only the uniformity of a super-church on the horizon. Moreover, this diversity is not characterized by a calm mood of sweetness and comraderie. At

These new Christian bodies shared at least two characteristics. First, in each country the reformers became aligned with the rising national consciousness, causing the dominant Protestant church to be "established," that is, officially recognized and given privileges by the government. The religious map of Europe was therefore colored with Lutheranism in Germany and Scandinavia, with the Reformed (Presbyterian) in Switzerland and Scotland and with Anglicanism in England. The Roman Catholic Church maintained its state privileges in Italy, Spain, France and elsewhere. Some Protestant groups came to be known as the "free churches" (those not established by the state) or pejoratively as "dissenters." Their ranks included the Congregationalists, Baptists and Presbyterians in England, the Anabaptists in Germany and many other varied groups. As a second common characteristic, each established church had its own confession, creed or polity, which defined the faith and set the boundaries of belonging and belief. Thus these European churches became known as "confessions," signifying that those who belonged shared a common history, theological consensus and church order.

When European Christians emigrated to America, a new form of the church developed, shaped by the environment of the new culture and democracy. The denomination was the organizational form of the religious freedom won by independence and guaranteed by the American Constitution's pledge for the separation of church and state. No church was legally established or blessed by the state; all were "free" —that is, able to develop as their religious convictions led them. The focus of the denomination, in contrast to other forms of the church, "is not primarily confessional, and it is certainly not territorial. Rather it is purposive.... It is, rather, a voluntary association of likehearted and like-minded individuals, who are united on the basis of common beliefs for the purpose of accomplishing tangible and defined objectives."[10]

According to Mead, the influences that contributed toward the shaping of American denominations—note these as important indicators for future ecumenical prospects — are (1) a "historylessness" that allows each denomination to justify its beliefs and practices as conforming more to the New Testament church than those of its rivals; (2) the voluntary principle, which defines the church as a voluntary association of like-minded individuals; (3) the vital place of the mission enterprise at home and overseas, prompted by pietism, which stresses personal religious experience and evangelization; (4) revivalism as a technique for evangelism and mission; (5) the churches' flight from reason to pietism with its nonintellectual, heart-religion approach; and (6) intense competition among the denominations. Seen in the light of the ecumenical question, these formative ingredients of early American Christianity help us understand why certain prospects for Christian unity are not joyously received among the folk. For example, the ecumenical movement talks about a God-given unity, but Americans tend to believe that their unity comes by their voluntary choice of each other. The ecumenical movement proposes a bringing together of institutional identities, but Americans see this as the diminishing of competition and of the choice of religious affiliation. The ecumenical movement requires hard theological discourse, which Americans tend to turn away from with an antiintellectual bias. Little wonder that the call to Christian unity seems alien.

As a form of church, the denomination has been blessed and cursed with no small amount of naïveté. Beyond Mead, other historians have appraised denominationalism as "the destiny which awaits the whole of the Catholic Church of the Future" (L.J. Trinterud),[11] the "basis for ecumenicity" (Winthrop Hudson),[12] an inevitable guarantor of religious freedom (W.E. Garrison)[13] or "a form of American indigenization" (Karl Hertz).[14] The seventeenth-century English dissenter Jeremiah Burroughes seems to speak for the vast number of lay folk in North America when he said that there have always been divisions in the church and "so long as we live here in this muddy world" there will continue to be division among the godly.[15]

The critics of denominations are equally vocal and passionate.[16] Two classic censures come from theologian H. Richard Niebuhr and from Charles Clayton Morrison, founding editor of *The Christian Century*. Niebuhr's *The Social Sources of Denominationalism* (1929) referred to denominationalism as "an unacknowledged hypocrisy." A divided church is utterly wrong, he said, primarily because it represents an ethical failure, "a compromise, made far too lightly, between Christianity and the world." His critique rings with a new relevance in light of recent world developments:

> It represents the accommodation of Christianity to the caste-system of human society. It carries over into the organization of the Christian principle of brotherhood the prides and prejudices, the privilege and prestige, as well as the humiliations and abasements, the injustices and inequalities of that specious order of high and low wherein men find the satisfaction of their craving for vainglory. The division of the churches closely follows the division of men into the castes of national, racial, and economic groups. It draws the color line in the church of God; it fosters the misunderstandings, the self exaltations, the hatreds

of jingoistic nationalism by continuing in the body of Christ the spurious differences of provincial loyalties; it seats the rich and poor apart at the table of the Lord, where the fortunate may enjoy the bounty they have provided while the others feed upon the crusts their poverty affords.[17]

In a later book, *The Kingdom of God in America* (1950), Niebuhr took a more positive view, recognizing both dynamism and unity in American Christianity. But he still viewed denominations as obstacles and improper institutionalizations of this dynamism. Indeed, the denominations marked the end of the dynamic movements in the church by becoming ends in themselves. There was no doubt in the Yale professor's mind that denominations stifle the dynamic unity of the church. The traditions became self-serving denominations rather than structures of the universal church.

A second classic critique of denominationalism came in Charles Clayton Morrison's Hoover Lectures at the University of Chicago, published as *The Unfinished Reformation* (1953). With characteristic Morrison fervor—and, some believed, naïve zeal—he denounced the denominational system in a list of sins:

1. Denominationalism is exceedingly and scandalously wasteful of the resources of Protestantism.

2. It is a shameful embarrassment to the missionary expansion of Christianity.

3. It frustrates the efforts of Protestantism to discharge the responsibility which the social gospel lays upon the Christian Church.

4. It provincializes Protestant mentality by erecting barriers against the free flow of Christian thought.

5. It breeds a subtle and corrosive moral insincerity among Protestant Christians.

6. It denies to the local church the Christian status, the breadth of outlook, the spiritual inspiration, and the richness of fellowship which is its birthright as a part of the ecumenical church.

7. It condemns the parish minister to adopt methods and appeals which appreciably stultify his ministerial self-respect as well as the Christian dignity of his high vocation.

8. Glorying in its false freedom denominationalism denies the freedom that is in Christ.[18]

Dr. Morrison is sometimes dismissed for his exaggerated statements, but he cuts through issues and catches an essential truth. Many of our denominational claims to distinctiveness are little more than veiled attempts to treat partial truths as dogma or final truth. This attitude has to be judged, corrected and made catholic by the wholeness of the gospel. His ultimate critique of the denomination was its "churchism," the assumption whereby it claims for itself those functions and purposes which "belong only to the unity of the whole Church of Christ."[19] Only together in that unity can Christians give an account of the faith and hope that is in us.

Thus far I have discussed critiques by two prominent First World, Western-thinking theologians. It is also important to listen to a Third World voice. Ironically, Asian-American theologian Roy I. Sano echoes Niebuhr but also relates denominationalism to the colonialism and oppression which the West imposes around the globe. Sano wrote in 1980:

What is offensive to Pacific and Asian Americans—and no doubt to other ethnic minorities, women, and the Third World—is that denominationalism is based on historic battles that are unrelated to their indigenous histories. Once denominational ties are established, we are recruited to do battle in the theology, liturgy, polity, and social stances. Acculturation into a resilient and resurgent denominationalism makes ethnic people pay the price of imported divisions in their communities. Commitments to their creative ecumenism are weakened.[20]

This questioning of the doctrine and mission of denominationalism by those seeking liberation, both theologically and culturally, is an important new ingredient in the debate.

Lesslie Newbigin, the revered missionary and bishop in the Church of South India, takes a similar negative position based on the missionary calling of the local congregation: denominational peculiarities are "separations that look to the past, which are determined not by the future hope that all shall be one, but by the past quarrels through which the Church is being divided, which takes out of the past not the one name of Jesus but other names by which the congregation is to be defined."[21]

Recently the whole debate over division and denominations has shifted ground in another direction, as seen in Dean R. Hoge's illuminating sociological study, *Division in the Protestant House* (1976). We face today, he says, tensions that are making American Christianity impotent and fragmented over new issues. The main schism is between private Protestantism (oriented toward revivalism and individual salvation) and public Protestantism (focusing on social problems and embracing a more liberal theology).[22] These pseudo-doctrines of the church have created new bases for division.

One conflict, apparent in all denominations today, centers on institutional priorities. Which programs will be highlighted and adequately funded? How will mission monies be spent? Factions within every church are at loggerheads as these decisions are considered; one faction argues for mission and social action, the other argues for evangelism and personal morality. "The real issue," however, says Hoge in a perceptive insight, "is whether social action, corporate or individual, supports white middle-class interests or appears to threaten those interests. . . . The main conflict over the social mission of the church thus turns out to be largely a conflict over maintaining or transcending white middle-class interests."[23]

A second deep conflict that now divides Christians in the United States, Canada and elsewhere comes from two distinct world views. One is theological and religious, with its center in the church; the other is scientific and humanistic, with its center in the academic community. This fragmentation leads to the exalting of technology and the devaluing of culture and morals.[24]

The sad fact about this polarization is that it makes it difficult, if not impossible, for society and the churches to communicate values and meaning to young and old, many of whom are today desperately turning to any cult or movement that will soothe their crisis of faith and meaning. In this context a traditional ecumenical adage takes on new significance: a divided church denies its message and weakens its mission. As far as the ecumenical future is concerned, Hoge offers two important points of counsel. First, we must realize that the basic causes of division are both social and theological, and any strategy toward Christian unity must so perceive and pursue the issues. Second, the real solutions to Christian divisions will not be achieved by actions at the political or organizational level. "The ailment of the Protestant Church is at the very core, and the healing must begin with the core questions—of religious truth and authentic life."[25] Unless we can recover the meanings of the Christian community and share those with society, all the political and structural maneuvers will bring little but temporary help.

Let us summarize this chapter's findings. Church unity cannot be conceived as a move away from diversity and toward a super-tribe, one people with homogenized identities. Diversity and variety are authentic gifts of a loving God, both for the human family and for the family which bears the name of Christ. But neither can diversity be a masquerade for selfishness or Christian separation according to racial, cultural or national status. Denominational structures may have been inevitable, but they are also provisional as communities of meaning. They can claim legitimacy only as they serve the search for full unity and manifested catholicity. Whenever denominations are expressions of exclusiveness they are sinful divisions.

Because we believe that God's saving love in Jesus Christ is commended to us and to all peoples, we are confident that all God's people can freely taste God's love. Moreover we have an assured hope that differences, whether natural or ecclesiological, can neither forestall nor ultimately hide the unity of the gospel. Diversity dynamically encompassed within authentic unity is the only goal worthy of Christ's church.

Such a church in Lanett, Alabama, and throughout the uttermost parts of the earth, would be a community of spiritual power; it would be worthy not only of its name but worthy of its mission.

2 Is There a Crisis in Christian Unity?

"Why are you writing a book on Christian unity? I thought that movement was dead." My friend's words touched a nerve. My first inclination was to counter his "ignorance" with an avalanche of information. I would tell him of the multitude of ecumenical activities of councils of churches (world, national, state), of forty united churches, church union conversations in over thirty countries, bilateral dialogues of all mixtures (Anglican-Roman Catholic, Lutheran-Presbyterian, Methodist-Orthodox, and so forth). I would tell him of the splendid witness of Church Women United, of global caring through Church World Service and of local ecumenical projects of infinite variety (Week of Prayer for Christian Unity, task forces on drugs among young people, joint eucharistic services, care of the elderly, joint evangelism, counseling for the unemployed, food delivered to the homebound). Somehow I resisted the temptation. His skepticism represents an attitude shared by many who have lost touch with or, indeed, have never experienced the ecumenical movement. They believe the rumors that the movement for Christian unity has slowed down, stalled or become archaic. The answer to my friend's question requires more than impressive data or impassioned pleas. The answer has something to do with the comprehensiveness of the Christian faith and with the reality of the whole church in the world.

Another friend speaks about the crisis of Christian unity from a totally different perspective. Gordon Gray is a Presbyterian minister in Northern Ireland, a country where two religious and cultural parties are engaged in guerrilla warfare. At the Nairobi Assembly of the World Council of Churches (1975), Gray was part of a panel of three persons who spoke about Christian unity from different contexts around the world. He shared the pain inflicted on his homeland by divisions in the church and the society. The Irish have learned that church divisions provide a breeding ground for other kinds of sectarianism that can tear a society apart. Then, speaking from this perspective, he concluded: "Divided churches cost lives."

Somewhere between the utterances of my two friends is the vital but complex dialogue about the unity of the people of God.

To say the ecumenical movement is in a time of crisis is not to confess anything necessarily profound or negative. A crisis need not reflect loss of effectiveness. Families facing deep crises often grow closer together and discover the stuff of their spiritual resources. Looking at the broad issues, I believe there are three dimensions to the ecumenical crisis.

First, the crisis over Christian unity is due to the spiritual uncertainty that marks Western civilization. Ours is a time of unexcelled achievements and capacities, of wealth, technology and knowledge. But a restless and disillusioned people show that these do not satisfy. It is a time of global commerce, communication and travel, all creating a new interdependence. But international interdependence does not create Christian or human unity. Interdependence creates thousands of new links, but it may also intensify our feelings of loneliness and alienation.

Ours is a time in which billions of dollars are spent on self-reflection and self-improvement, yet everywhere we read the signs of a crisis of identity in persons and institutions. It is a time of reclaimed pluralism in culture, language, ethnic heritage and political persuasion, yet society seems to lack any principle of cohesion, teetering on the brink of disintegration. Uncertain about who we are, distrusting the institutions that touch our lives, confused about the grounds of our hope — we ourselves are signs of the times. In times such as these, people are not encouraged to search for ways to bind men and women and churches together in unity, in love and in peace. Yet in such times the ecumenical movement finds its greatest reason for its work by calling the churches to their urgent and fundamental mission to become a living sign of fellowship and hope.

Second, if the movement toward Christian unity is in crisis, it is a crisis of *growth*. The churches have moved so far that they have not been able to find the ecumenical patterns that express their emerging unity and that liberate Christians for service in the world. The crisis

is really like a child still taking its first exploratory steps or perhaps a teen-age youngster awkwardly moving into a future he can only dimly foresee. If there is disappointment in today's ecumenical scene, that is due, partly at least, to our expecting too much too soon. It takes far more than occasional spurts of enthusiasm to create an institutional pattern that will provide the right balance of unity and diversity in the church after centuries of fragmentation. Those who expect "instant ecumenicity" and are discouraged when they do not see it have little understanding of the way in which meaningful social advance is made.[1]

In reality, today's ecumenical crisis is due to those tensions that are inevitably sparked when an ideal begins to be translated into the lives of people and their institutions. The progress achieved over the past seven decades has produced a startling range of new problems and issues, all of which signal that the era of superficial relations is past. Now the churches are required to make hard commitments. We have entered the era of costly ecumenism. The growth toward unity can only come through pain, through tough dialogue and decisions. Christian unity viewed as sweetness and light is passé, but unity that comes through struggling together with what it means to be Christian and human in this messy world—that sort of movement has hardly begun.

Finally, the crisis of the ecumenical movement is fundamentally a reflection of the crisis of the *churches*. The hesitancies or the lack of firm commitment to full unity are but symptoms of internal conflicts, the faith crises, institutional survival pangs, uncertainties with an alien society *within* the particular churches—Roman Catholic, Protestant or Orthodox. It is important to acknowledge that the critical state of the ecumenical movement at this moment is an essential part of its life and vitality; Christian unity and ecumenism will always be in such a crisis. In the final analysis, a crisis is the occasion for making important and decisive choices about the present and the future. Making those choices and decisions requires a clear head about the changing world in which we live and the kind of community we are called to be.

WHAT MAKES UNITY SO DIFFICULT?

When we are honest with ourselves we can uncover a long list of resistances to unity. Their number is far greater and their causes are far deeper than most people are willing to admit. This is not the place to catalog or to give a commentary on all of them. Yet honest seekers after unity must know and face them.

The most powerful barriers to unity are *psychological*. They come from fear—fear of losing cherished beliefs and practices in our own traditions, fear of changes we do not understand, fear of uniformity. Such fears cannot be lightly dismissed; beneath them are deep feelings involving our self-images, our goals, our hopes. So when a person says, "I am for unity, but not for uniformity," that person not only reveals a judgment on a particular ecumenical model, but also says something fundamental about his or her personal pilgrimage. The irony is that the documentary history shows that every ecumenical conference from the beginning has denounced uniformity and claimed unity-in-diversity as the future goal to be sought. Every description of unity and every plan of union speaks of a unity that contains far more diversity than now exists within any Christian tradition or denomination. The testimony of councils of churches and united churches gives the same evidence: in unity the distinctive gifts of the traditions are not lost but enriched. Fear of Christian unity tells us a great deal about a more fundamental uncertainty, however. An individual's crisis of identity makes the acceptance of a neighbor's reconciling love very difficult. So also with the individual churches: if they are uncertain about who they are and where they are going, a future that calls for them to converge naturally looks foreboding, something to fear.

Another category of resistances to unity is *sociological*. The prospects of Christian unity are affected, for example, by class differences. Even in the celebrated Church of South India, congregations are divided by languages and class structures. When consideration is being given in a particular country to uniting two nearby congregations or electing the steering committee for a local mission project, it is not uncommon to hear the excuse: "But *they* are not *our* kind of people." Too many people want the churches to be "happy and comfortable," like a social club. They want the churches to grow, to be successful in numbers, wealth and prestige. To achieve this "success" they are unwilling to take the risks of sharing life with those of different social classes, races or life experiences. True catholicity eludes them; they choose disunity.

Other factors that influence a lukewarm attitude toward the ecumenical movement lie in the realm of *history and theology*. Hard issues of Christian faith and practice still tragically divide the churches. We cannot deny these theological differences—ministry, sacraments, creeds, biblical authority; they are part and parcel of our divided churches as well as causes for anxiety in the search for unity. They represent deep issues of faith and life. But the manner in which we handle these issues is critical. If protecting our historical position on baptism or bishops or elders or whatever becomes only a defense mechanism for protecting our tradition, then theology becomes self-serving, not gospel-proclaiming. Theology becomes demonic when people are unwilling to reconsider historical factors or theological positions that once shaped their lives and beliefs.

Out of fear of losing their denominational identity, Christians cling fiercely to old identities expressed in terms of outdated theological issues. Our identity becomes a myth if we take a theological issue from the past and rebaptize it "our denominational witness." In ecumenical dialogue we are constantly learning that some theological issues have become smokescreens for other problems that rarely surface on the agenda of the churches. For example, divergences about ministry—episcopal or nonepiscopal, clergy or laity—have behind them historical memories nurtured by the fathers and mothers of previous generations. Some nonepiscopal churches suspect bishops "like the ones Anglicans had in the seventeenth century," but the truth of the matter may be that these churches have as many, if not more, autocratic tendencies as churches that supposedly have a different theology of ministry and governance. Such biases keep many Christians from understanding the proper place of pastoral oversight in the church, and thus from being open to proposals for reconciling the traditions.

Theological issues can be signs of the past or carriers of an ecumenical future. W.A. Visser 't Hooft, the first general secretary of the World Council of Churches, once said: "If we consider our positions, not as fortresses to be defended, but rather as temporary resting-places from which we are to journey onward, we find that other confessions represent truths through which we must let ourselves be questioned, called to order and corrected. And what is more, it may happen that we come to understand that somehow we are already one in Christ, in spite of all that seems to stand between us."[2]

This brief survey of the sources of hesitancy toward unity should include the failures of ecumenical strategists and ecumenical bodies. The ecumenical movement is often long on euphoria and short on clarity. We seem able to announce the imperative to unity with holy fire, but unable to give a clear idea of what visible Christian unity looks like and of how it can be achieved. An Eastern Orthodox who gave deeply to the ecumenical movement made this critique of himself and others:

> If we turn to the testimony of those who take part in the Ecumenical Movement, we generally find that it has one common feature: there is a startling discrepancy between the value which they attach to their

23

experience, often speaking of it with enthusiasm, and the extreme poverty of its content, or at any rate their utter inability to express the fullness of it in words. They describe their experience as a miracle, a revelation, almost a new birth; but when questioned as to the content of that revelation, they answer with what may appear as platitudes or self-evident truths.[3]

Such critiques, however, can only be made by those who are willing to give their lives to the task of making the vision of unity clear and discovering ways for unity to become a daily experience for Christians. Other faults of ecumenical strategists and ecumenical bodies might be admitted: the preoccupation with institutional models of unity to the detriment of spiritual relations, the lack of love for those who oppose the movement, our versions of "sectarian ecumenism" ("if you don't agree with us you are damned"), and the projection of an image that ecumenism is what happens in bureaucratic and administrative programs. These cause people to look upon the ecumenical movement with suspicion, and rightly so.

All of the foregoing fears and causes of hesitation, plus a host of others that could be discussed, contribute to the ups and downs of the ecumenical movement. But rational answers will not necessarily overcome them. As Father Michael Hurley observes:

> Fears are not exorcized by reason, nor is one fear to be counteracted by arousing another and a greater. Our fear of ecumenism will be overcome therefore neither by logic nor by a counterbalancing fear of the disaster to Christianity which must result from skulking alone in a sectarian cave of isolationism. The real remedy for our ecumenical fear is the creative force of good example. That would seem to be sound theology as well as sound psychology.[4]

An important clue is found in those words. Our answers to the fearful, the lukewarm and the hostile will make an impact only if we show forth living examples of what reconciling love means. In ecumenism, the imperative must become the indicative. Unity is served not only by ecumenical models but by ecumenical persons.

THE MEANINGS OF "ECUMENICAL"

It is important to take note of the various meanings that are applied to the word *ecumenical*. Otherwise its meaning will become mushy and the word will be used in vague ways that imply little more than goodwill or friendliness toward others.

Ecumenical comes from the Greek word *oikoumene,* which means "the whole inhabited world." Like most Christian words it was first a secular word that came to be invested with new meaning. Its roots are in the Greek noun *oikos* (house; hence a household or family), and the verb *oikeo* (to live or to dwell). For the Greeks, the *oikoumene* meant the civilized world where Greek culture reigned and held people together. For the Romans, the *oikoumene* was identified with the Empire, where Roman law and imperial power decided the boundaries. In due time the New Testament writers began to use the word. Luke, for example, starts the account of the birth of Jesus by saying: "In those days a decree went out from Caesar Augustus that all the *oikoumene* (world) should be enrolled" (Luke 2:1). Then in that powerful description of the early Christians in Thessalonica: "These men who have turned the *oikoumene* upside down have come here also" (Acts 17:6). In some early uses, the reference was to the Roman Empire, that is, to the known world; on other occasions the word referred to the universal human community. Matthew wrote: "And this gospel of the kingdom will be preached throughout the whole *oikoumene,* as a testimony to all nations" (Matt. 24:14).

In the early centuries of the church, *ecumenical* begins to be used to represent the church as a whole, the universal church. Councils whose decisions were accepted as authoritative throughout the whole church (Nicea, Constantinople and so forth) and creeds that were generally accepted (Apostles', Nicene and Athanasian) were described as ecumenical.[5]

When the modern ecumenical movement began, its pioneers adopted the ancient term *ecumenical* as its self-portrait. They then proceeded to give new perspectives to its meaning. The first person to use the term widely in the twentieth century was Archbishop Nathan Söderblom of Uppsala (Sweden). His usage, especially on the eve of World War I, signified the essential oneness of all Christians in the midst of denominational divisions and international conflict. From then on the word enjoyed widespread currency among the churches. For Söderblom "the word contains far more than the connotation of universal representation. He poured into it the whole content of his conviction concerning the basic unity of the Christian Church and its common task in the world."[6] In all languages it became the popular signature of this worldwide fellowship searching for full unity in Christ. In French, for example, World Council of Churches is translated *Conseil Oecuménique des Eglises* and in German, *Oekumenischer Rat der Kirchen.*

In this modern usage the word *ecumenical* carries three distinct but interrelated meanings.

CHRISTIAN UNITY: MATRIX FOR MISSION

1. Ecumenical means a concern for *the visible unity of the church*. At the Oxford Conference of Life and Work (1937), Orthodox and Protestants declared: The term ecumenical refers to the expression within history of the given unity of the church. The thought and action of the church are ecumenical, in so far as they attempt to realize the *Una Sancta,* the fellowship of Christians, who acknowledge the one Lord.[7] For Protestants, Orthodox and Roman Catholics the word has come to signify their desire to manifest the God-given unity denied by their divisions. Oliver Tomkins, the Anglican bishop of Bristol and a World Council of Churches leader for many years, says that "the word 'ecumenical' is used to denote interest in Christian unity and church unity."[8] Vatican II's *Decree on Ecumenism* makes two references to the meaning of ecumenical, both of which lift up the centrality of the unity of Christians:

> God has begun to bestow more generously upon divided Christians remorse over their divisions and a longing for unity ... there increases from day to day a movement, fostered by the grace of the Holy Spirit, for the restoration of unity among all Christians. Taking part in this movement, which is called ecumenical, are those who invoke the Triune God and confess Jesus as Lord and Savior. (Article 1)

> The "ecumenical movement" means those activities and enterprizes which, according to various needs of the Church and opportune occasions, are started and organized for the fostering of unity among Christians. (Article 4)

2. Ecumenism means the church *reaching out in its worldwide mission*. To continue with the insights found in the *Decree on Ecumenism:* "Almost everyone, though in different ways, longs that there may be one visible Church of God, a Church truly universal and sent forth to the whole world that the world may be converted to the gospel and so be saved, to the glory of God" (Article 1). Here the ecumenical responsibility of the church involves going into the whole inhabited world to witness in faith to Jesus Christ. John A. Mackay, the great missionary statesman, gave this emphasis to our word:

> A true "Ecumenical Movement" must have at the heart of it the dynamic expression of a pre-existing unity in Christ which, being missionary in character, strives to express itself throughout the entire *oikoumene,* that is, both in the world of church relations and in the secular order. The crucial awareness on the part of Christians of their unity in Christ must lead them to be missionary-minded in loyalty to Christ, that [hu]mankind may be brought to his allegiance.[9]

CRISIS IN CHRISTIAN UNITY?

A further clarification of this meaning came as early as 1951, just three years after the constituting assembly of the World Council of Churches. Members of the Central Committee meeting in Rolle, Switzerland, were concerned about the trend among some people to focus on either unity or mission, thus dividing its two primary emphases. To avoid this danger they issued an historic statement entitled "The Calling of the Church to Mission and to Unity," which says in part:

> We would especially draw attention to the recent confusion in the use of the word "ecumenical." It is important to insist that this word, which comes from the Greek word for the whole inhabited earth, is properly used to describe everything that relates to *the whole task of the whole Church to bring the Gospel to the whole world.* It therefore *covers equally the missionary movement and the movement towards unity,* and must not be used to describe the latter in contradistinction to the former. We believe that a real service will be rendered to true thinking on these subjects in the Churches if we so use this word that it *covers both Unity and Mission in the context of the whole world.*

> Thus the obligation to take the Gospel to the whole world (mission), and the obligation to draw all Christ's people together (unity) both rest upon Christ's whole work, and are indissolubly connected. Every attempt to separate these two tasks violates the wholeness of Christ's ministry to the world. Both of them are, in the strictest sense of the word, essential to the being of the Church and the fulfilment of its function as the Body of Christ.[10]

The dual focus upon these two is necessary to grasp the deeper meanings of the ecumenical life.

3. A third perspective, which is an extension of the first two, has lately been associated with the word ecumenical. It is now used to speak of the *unity of the church as a sign of the unity of humankind.* At the Uppsala (1968) and Nairobi (1975) assemblies of the World Council of Churches this insight was articulated and accepted. The clearest reflections on this direction, however, came in a paper from the Accra, Ghana, meeting of the Faith and Order Commission in 1974. This perspective puts concern for church unity sharply in the wider context of humanity. "In pursuing our quest for the visible unity of the Church, we are seeking the fulfillment of God's purpose as it is declared to us in Jesus Christ. This purpose concerns the world, the whole of [hu]mankind, and the whole of created order."[11] In this emphasis *mission* includes working to enable "the just interdependence of free people," and *unity* reaches its deepest expression

27

as we live in solidarity with those engaged in the struggles for liberation, justice and equality. A particular nuance of this definition of ecumenical permits conflict if it is necessary to bring Christ's liberating spirit. Ecumenical refers to a "unity in tension."

Finally, a few clarifications are necessary in order to keep our understandings of ecumenism from becoming dispersed into insignificance. If it applies to everything, it means nothing. The first abuse can be in what W.A. Visser 't Hooft calls the danger of "an ecumenical inflation." Unfortunately, ecumenical is a quality claimed for practically everything the churches do, worthwhile or worthless. Nevertheless ecumenical is not synonymous with interdenominational or cooperative; nor is a project or event necessarily ecumenical because Lutherans, Presbyterians, Methodists and Baptists are working together, or because Roman Catholics, Pentecostalists and Orthodox sit at a banquet together. To be ecumenical means that in some credible sense the universal mission of Christ is served, and the unity experienced is a unity that binds Christians together visibly in Christ's presence.

Furthermore, ecumenical, rightly defined, centers in Jesus Christ. It is not an apt word for the dialogue in which Christians engage with Jews, Muslims, Buddhists and people of other living faiths and ideologies. Such dialogue is a timely and critical responsibility of the churches. It ranks in the highest of priorities in light of the world situation. But the accurate use of language and the integrity of the ecumenical movement require us to speak of this as an interreligious or interfaith dialogue. The distinction is more than semantic. Historically, the word ecumenical has a Christian basis, and any careless use of it gives the erroneous impression that ecumenically minded persons do not care about theological convictions.

The balancing of these three meanings of ecumenical—concern for Christian unity, mission and the unity of humankind—gives us the content and the context for the pilgrimage to which Christ has called us. These meanings give us the standards for testing our work and searching toward the fullness of the gospel. The task of the churches is for "the whole Church to bring the whole Gospel to the whole world." Our faithfulness is, therefore, a concrete calling to visible unity in the fulfillment of mission for the sake of humanity.

3 Unity: The Biblical Perspective

Earlier generations in search of church unity turned instinctively to the Bible. And so must we. Finding out what the Bible says about unity, however, is not a simple problem with easy solutions. At the very beginning we face difficulties, one arising from the times in which we live and the other from the New Testament itself.

THE CRISIS OF BIBLICAL AUTHORITY

Our task is confounded, first, by a modern-day crisis in biblical authority. Many people today simply do not accept the Bible as authoritative. Their signals for life come from other "authorities"— science, personal experience, sports or the mass media. This crisis has led to what James D. Smart calls "the strange silence of the Bible in the Church." "The voice of the Scriptures is falling silent in the preaching and teaching of the Church and the consciousness of Christian people, a silence that is perceptible even among those who are most insistent upon their devotion to the Scriptures."[1] Any understanding of church unity from a biblical perspective is, therefore, blocked by the fact that the fundamental Scriptures are considered irrelevant by many and ignored by others. Many highly sophisticated persons today tend to relegate the Bible and its world to the category of antiquities.

The second problem is the nature of the biblical community, or at least, how it is perceived. Most Christians now agree that it is impossible to find in the Bible a blueprint or a single normative pattern for the church that can be "restored" or reproduced to establish the church's unity. Despite the claims of the "restorationists," who see in the New Testament a perfectly united church (which

29

usually resembles their own church!), or the claims of the "early catholics," who identify only *one* developing trend of creed, ministry and sacraments, the Christian community of the New Testament actually reveals a variety of thought and practice. To say this does not diminish the importance of the primitive church; it only keeps us from making idealized judgments about the church in the first century and from constructing a preconceived, prepackaged formula about the nature of Christian unity. The primitive church struggled, as we must, for unity.

UNITY IN THE OLD TESTAMENT

A biblical perspective on Christian unity begins not with the New Testament but with the Old Testament or Hebrew Scriptures. As the early Christians seem to have realized far better than we, the church of the New Testament was not an entirely new creation; rather, it was the heir of the Old Testament.[2]

From beginning to end the Old Testament story is one of alienation and reconciliation, brokenness and restored unity. In creation, as told in the Book of Genesis, God wills for the world peace, harmony and fruitfulness. God creates humanity as a community of men and women, a vision of human unity based on obedient and joyful service to God. "And God saw everything that he had made, and behold, it was very good" (Gen. 1:31). God's creatures were meant to live in communion with God and with one another.

Before long Adam and Eve rebelled and broke their fellowship with God. By claiming for themselves equality with God, they destroyed the childlike trust that keeps men and women open to God's love and to one another. The lust for power caused them to lose their at-one-ness with God. But God forgave them and gave them life despite their disobedience. As a consequence of the broken relationship between Creator and creature, Cain, the firstborn of Eve, murders his brother Abel (Genesis 4), and again human corruption and sin thwart God's loving purpose. Yet God does not totally forsake the murderer. Cain leaves God's presence, but God does not lose sight of Cain: God never allows hatred and destruction to be victorious.

After the great flood, symbolizing the cleansing of the human race, God made a covenant with Noah and his family. The rainbow was sent as a guarantee that never again would God deal with the human family in that way. Again, God's judgment was followed by God's grace.

Later, God was made sorrowful by the tower of Babel episode (Genesis 11). A self-serving people said: "Come, let us build ourselves a city, and a tower with its top in the heavens, and let us make a name for ourselves, lest we be scattered abroad upon the face of the whole earth" (Gen. 11:4). This construction project reflected a blatant lust for power. The people, in their own pride and power, attempted to create a false unity to make a name for themselves. The result was disorder and separation from God, but again God promises humanity another kind of unity.

These biblical stories tell again and again how the divine intention of communion is frustrated. Goodness and grace are met with acts of violence and rebellion as people turn from God's redeeming purpose and face destruction.

God's reconciling purpose is symbolized next in one people. In a new covenant with Abraham, God created a new nation (Genesis 12, 15). Israel was to be the instrument of unity, with a mission to bring God's healing to all humanity. But the people of Israel lost sight of this mission. God established a covenant with Moses, the powerful Hebrew who grew up in the Egyptian court, but again Israel broke the covenant through pride and a rebellious spirit. Covenants were established for the purpose of uniting humanity, but some always chose to live in rebellion.

The tragedy of a rebellious Israel which broke its covenants is the central motif of the prophets. God's chosen people were an unfaithful people; God's redemptive purpose was unfulfilled even in the lives of God's servant people. Yet the prophets tried to call the people back from humiliation and division to their vocation of unity and mission for the world. Second Isaiah's "servant songs" tell in lyrical form of the Israelites' twofold calling of unity and mission: to restore the broken unity of Israel and to be a light to the nations that God's healing salvation may reach the end of the earth (Isa. 49:5-6). Ezekiel and Hosea similarly brought judgment to this unfaithful people, but also offered the divine promise of reconciliation. God's calling and promises were given to a remnant, a small group of the faithful who became the community that witnessed to God's redeeming love for all humanity.

The Old Testament story of the people of Israel illustrates the relentless witness of God to the importance of unity for the fulfillment of the mission of the servant people. The unity that exists within the life of Israel itself is the essence of Israel's witness to the nations. God's ecumenical purpose is, therefore, revealed in "the 'stubbornness' of God's love for a blessed and united [hu]mankind which outlasts the stubborn repetition of human sin and repentance."[3]

DIVERSITY AND DISUNITY
IN THE EARLY CHURCH

As soon as we turn to the church in the New Testament, we find any romantic illusions of a perfect community disappearing. C.H. Dodd rightly insists that "the governing idea in the New Testament is that of the one Church—a unique society constituted by an act of God in history."[4] We must confess, however, that a lot of silly sentiment has been written and spoken about the golden unity of spirit and practice in early Christianity that fails to recognize the deep differences, even hostilities, that already existed. The unity of the early Christians was blessed with diversity, strained with tensions and even threatened by deep divisions between important leaders and contending groups.[5]

In the early 1940s, E.F. Scott pointed to the naturalness of diversity in his study of "the varieties of New Testament religion."[6] The new faith spread throughout the known world and took root in the soils of different cultures. Persons of different temperaments who lived in different situations believed, taught and interpreted the faith. If you compare the books of the New Testament — the Synoptic Gospels (Matthew, Mark and Luke) with John, or Romans with James, or Matthew with Paul's epistles—you will find a wide range of theology (including diverse interpretations of Christ), concepts of ministry, patterns of worship, understanding of the sacraments of baptism and the Lord's Supper and approaches to politics. Only one who is obsessed with a self-justifying theory will miss the essential, enriching diversity among New Testament Christians, and be blind to the genuine unity to which this diversity testifies.

This diversity also broke into tensions and conflicts, which plagued the early church. The dominant ones related to geography and theology. For example, socioeconomic factions developed in Corinth over the Lord's Supper. The more prestigious members of the community came early to the Supper, which was preceded by a potluck dinner, whereas the poor and those who had to work longer hours arrived too late to eat (1 Cor. 11:17-34). Tensions arose between Peter and Paul (Gal. 2:11-14), and later between Paul and James; a dispute developed over ecclesiastical authority between the Elder of 2 John and Diotrephes "who likes to put himself first" (3 John 9). Jealousy developed between residents of Jerusalem and Antioch over which was the headquarters of the Christian church. Loyalty to particular personalities in Corinth — Paul, Apollos and Cephas (Peter)—contributed to disunity (1 Cor. 1:11-14).

Nor was the apostolic church without theological controversies, which sometimes seemed intractable. Beyond the so-called heresies (which carried such technical names as gnosticism and docetism), we see serious conflicts over the meaning of Christ, or over who belongs to the fellowship, or over ethical questions. A classic divergence developed between the Jewish Christians (who believed that disciples first had to follow the Jewish laws and customs) and the Hellenist Christians (converted Jews scattered by the Diaspora who spoke Greek and accepted Greek customs). Bitter competition between Paul and Peter and between Antioch (Hellenist) and Jerusalem (Jewish) gives evidence that deeper distinctions existed between these Christians. This hot conflict was played out in three dramatic events in the life of the young church. The martyrdom of Stephen, a Hellenist who was persecuted, brought controversy. The apostolic council between Paul and pillars of the church in Jerusalem had a contested agenda dealing with whether Gentiles had to submit to the Jewish religious practice of circumcision in order to become Christians. Peter's controversial visit to Antioch, where he ate with Gentile Christians, angered many of the brothers and sisters.[7]

A very different sort of conflict was the controversy between Paul and his lovable but contentious flock at Corinth. His concern for them caused Paul to write the letters we know as 1 and 2 Corinthians, to make an urgent emergency trip to Corinth and later to send his associate Titus. The issue was Christology: who is Jesus Christ, and for whom did he come, die and rise again? In the light of such tensions we can understand why some New Testament scholars speak of the unity and fellowship of the primitive church, not in euphoric phrases, but as "a solidarity of differences" (Ernst Käsemann).

But mark this: *none* of these conflicts and tensions parallel those found in the divided and dividing churches of today. Robert McAfee Brown states the truth forcefully: "By no stretch of the imagination can we find in the New Testament a justification for our present denominations and competing Christian groups. The impulse there is not an impulse towards divisiveness but towards unity. The notion of denominations, let alone huge *blocs* of Christians severed from full unity with each other, is foreign to its pages."[8]

In other words, diversity did not become schism in the New Testament period. Paul and Peter remained loyal to the same church. Across conflicts and theological chasms, Christians lived in eucharistic fellowship, welcomed one another's members, mutually accepted one another's ministries and acted in compassion toward one another's suffering. This is illustrated by Paul's collection of money from the Gentile churches for the poverty-stricken saints in Jerusalem. The New Testament presents neither an idealized, undivided church nor a church characterized by schisms like those of later centuries. It presents a church of unity in diversity. This is the first lesson to be learned from the conflicts and disunity of the early church.

The second lesson has to do with the ecumenical task. Our acceptance of an ecclesiology of the New Testament that contains threatening diversities and contradictory positions in theology, in organization and in devotional practice does not in any way lessen the urgency of the movement toward deeper, more visible unity. To recognize these diversities and conflicts, claims German New Testament Professor Ernst Käsemann, is "a great comfort" and "a theological gain." "For, in so doing, we come to see that our own history is one with that of primitive Christianity. Today, too, God's Spirit hovers over the waters of a chaos out of which divine creation is to take place."[9] This means that in a certain sense our age, too, is an apostolic age. Neither the early Christians nor we today are perfect examples of unity. We know the coming united church lies not in our past, but in our present and future, as we take our places among the pilgrim people moving toward the Kingdom of God.

BIBLICAL IMAGES OF THE CHURCH

While the church in the New Testament did not fully manifest unity, its members did believe Christ wills unity for those who are baptized into his body. They are called to share life. The witness to this truth is most clearly seen through the images and metaphors used to describe the church.

The New Testament writers knew that the vision of faith is more adequately expressed in images than in logical concepts. The great biblical metaphors are colorful pictures that tell what the church is like. Paul S. Minear's definitive study, *Images of the Church in the New Testament,* identified ninety-six of them,[10] all of which give a far more dynamic sense of the term *church* than common definitions that refer to buildings or denominations. These images stretch and focus our vision of the church and its unity.[11]

The New Testament speaks of the church as the *people of God,* an image brought back into greater usage by Vatican Council II (1962-1965). "Once you were no people but now you are God's people," declared the writer of 1 Peter (2:10a). In a similar vein, the church is described as the people of the *new covenant* (Gal. 6:16; Rom. 9:6-7; Heb. 8:8,10), the chosen of God (1 Peter 1:2; 2:9). This set of images links the early church with the covenant community of the Hebrew people. The 1 Peter passage also gives us another profound insight into the church's nature and witness:"Once you had not received mercy but now you have received mercy" (2:10b). God's people are brought into being — formed — by the mercy and forgiveness God gives. They are a new people, not by their merits or goodness, but by God's mercy to the "no people" of the world. Those who belong to God have a mission to be merciful to "those who sit in darkness."

The image of the church as a *flock* pervades the whole Bible. Because of the rural setting of Israel, the people are recognized on numerous occasions as God's sheep, and God in turn is the shepherd (Psalm 23; Isa. 40:11). Jesus used this vivid image to describe his own role in the parable of the shepherd (Matt. 18:12-14; Luke 15:2-7) and in responding to the Canaanite woman whose daughter was possessed by a demon: "I was sent only to the lost sheep of the house of Israel" (Matt. 15:24). In Hebrews Jesus Christ is portrayed as "the great shepherd of the sheep" (13:20). In the Gospel of John we find a most intimate description of unity and mission, symbolized in the relationship of the one flock and its one shepherd. "And I have other sheep, that are not of this fold; I must bring them also, and they will heed my voice. So there shall be one flock, one shepherd" (John 10:16). While John's basic point here has to do with the role of the shepherd (Christ), he nevertheless implies something about the church, too. Sheep cannot live alone. They must be together for protection under the shepherd.

The New Testament depicts the church as a building "built upon the foundation of the apostles and prophets, Christ Jesus himself being the chief cornerstone" (Eph. 2:20). It is "a holy temple in the Lord" (Eph. 2:21). Here we should not forget the meaning of a metaphor. It is not a literal description but rather, a picture that conveys meaningful insights. Hence, the temple referred to by the apostles was a worshiping, believing, witnessing community of persons, rather than a building of brick, limestone or wood. As 1 Peter says, each person (or manifestation of the church) is a *living* stone built into "a spiritual house" (2:5), which is a sign of God's presence with the people. Without each stone or brick the building is not whole. The church is "a living family, a fellowship created and sustained by the Holy Spirit." A person or group of persons destroys God's temples "not by acts which injure or harm a building, but by jealousies which divide the community."[12]

35

As the new temple, the church also assumes the formation of a new, holy priesthood (1 Peter 2:9; Rev. 1:6; 5:10; 20:6). Using the language of Old Testament offices, the New Testament writers proceeded to fill them with radical new meanings. The new priesthood was not the set-apart ministry of a few but the calling of *all* who love Christ to give their lives as a spiritual sacrifice, in loving, reconciling service to God and others (Rom. 12:1-2).

An image whose richness is not always appreciated is that of the church as *the bride of Christ* and Christ as the royal bridegroom (Eph. 5:21-33). Maybe this metaphor is neglected because it occurs in a section of the letter where Paul is discussing the relationship between a husband and wife—a description strongly rejected by many Christians today who see marriage as a partnership, not a submission. Yet with the image of the bride the writer of Ephesians is talking about the church in a profound way. The image he uses expresses "the astounding love which impelled the Bridegroom to come down from heaven, to humble himself to the level of his creation, that, in uniting himself to humanity, he might raise humanity to the heaven from which he came."[13] A church, like a marriage, in which love reigns supreme and which understands its mandate to bring all humanity to God's self-giving purpose would be a powerful church.

The image of the church most fully presented in the New Testament, and the one too easily belabored in church circles, is *the body of Christ*. Paul uses it constantly, and applies it to all sorts of situations. It appears most frequently in 1 Corinthians (6:5; 10:16-17; 11:29 and especially 12:12-31), but also fits into the messages of Romans (12:4-5), Colossians (1:18; 2:9-10), and Ephesians (1:22-23; 4:4-13; 5:23).

The body metaphor serves us best in grasping what the life of the Christian community ought to be in its insights related to unity and diversity. The *organic* character of the relationship between Christ and his church, and the members of the church with one another, is stressed. Our unity centers in Christ. The church is not simply an association of individuals, but nothing less than Christ himself living in the community. The community—its structures, its activities, its membership directories — is secondary to the special presence of Christ, made known particularly in baptism and the Lord's Supper.

This image strikes hard at our American view of the church as a collection of individuals. The church, it seems, depends on us; Christ is an occasional visitor. But this is not so, if the church is the body of Christ. Furthermore, this metaphor gives us particular insight into the place of individual parts. Paul makes clear the required interdependence of the members, using the parts of the body as an illustration. The eye cannot say to the hand, "I have no need of you." The fullness of life is achieved only when all members of the body are healthy and contribute to the life of the whole. Likewise, unity is not the sum total of our diversities. On the contrary, our diversities are valid only to the extent that they serve Christ and Christ's unity. This is not merely a rhapsodic vision of the church—though it surely is that —but a practical proposal for the way the church operates. It is as down-to-earth as sacramental practices, budgets and the roles assumed by church leaders.

This brief treatment of the images of the church in the New Testament should have revealed one element that is common to all of them: unity belongs to the very essence and vocation of the church. Community and communion are created by God's act in Christ. Jesus Christ is the center of the united church's life and service. The relationship between Christ and the church is dynamic, organic (knit together). The church is a model for *koinonia,* a unity that manifests love. It is a community whose unity is for the sake of reconciling all humanity.

THE VISION THROUGH EXEGESIS IN LIFE

Beyond the biblical images, we finally can appreciate the view— or better, views—of the church's unity in other passages of the New Testament by observing several different situations where the apostles, often in moving language, teach us something about the nature of unity in Christ. Let us reflect on several classic passages about Christian unity—Acts 2, Ephesians 4 and John 17. And do not forget our earlier reality test: namely, that the actual situation these texts reflect is not an idyllic unity but divergences on the brink of disunity. About all that held the participants together at times, apart from the grace of God, was their dogged will to remain one in the Body.

Luke's concept of unity, found in the second chapter of the Acts of the Apostles (vs. 42), reflects the afterglow of Pentecost. His portrait of Christian life in the "mother church" in Jerusalem is painted with the brush strokes of flexibility and unity, both signs of the newborn community. The miracle of Pentecost was the miracle of unity. It was God's dramatic cancellation of Babel, when the lust for power had thwarted communications and fractured fellowship among God's people and when differences of language, race and nation were allowed to isolate rather than to enrich. Babel led to a tearing apart of those who were originally created to live in harmony. At Pentecost such diverse and disparate people, from all the countries of the inhabited earth (*oikoumene*), became one people of God, living with Christ's spirit in their midst. A new ordering of life was given through the Resurrection. The church was born and became a community that draws people together in the kind of unity that makes it possible to overcome the forces of hatred and isolation that would destroy them.

Luke summarizes this unity, admittedly in rather romantic tones: "And they devoted themselves to the apostles' teaching and fellowship, to the breaking of bread and the prayers" (Acts 2:42). This fourfold activity simply presented the daily routine of Jewish Christians in the first century—certainly nothing that would make headlines in the *Jerusalem Times*. The power word for Luke, however, is "fellowship" (*koinonia*). Actually fellowship is too mild a translation to express its deep meaning of intimate communion, participation in one another's suffering. We may best translate *koinonia* as "common life"[14]—understanding, however, that for these early Christians *koinonia* has several aspects in addition to the four which Luke records, including having "one heart and soul," living in the same hope, even sharing property and material goods. This togetherness meant much more than that the early Christians belonged to the same organization or lived in the same city or neighborhood. They shared a spiritual togetherness expressive of a unity that could break down the barriers between Jews and Gentiles, that had an inner life which was expressed by an outgoing concern for others in compassion and self-sacrifice. This *koinonia* was, for Luke, the heart of Christian unity.

The letter to the Ephesians includes several classical passages concerning the meaning of Christian unity. Scholars are uncertain whether Paul was the author of this epistle, but the thought clearly is Pauline, bearing his metaphor of the body of Christ as well as his high doctrine of Christian unity. In the first chapter the letter describes the ecumenical scope of God's eternal purpose for creation, sealed by Christ: "to unite all things in him, things in heaven and things on earth" (1:10). In the next chapter we are told that the power of reconciliation is in the Cross of Christ, a unity powerful enough to reconcile both Jews and Gentiles—perhaps the most vivid hatred in human history—"in one body through the cross, thereby bringing the hostility to an end" (Eph. 2:16). In other Pauline passages this "peace" holds together in the church the strong and the weak, the famous and the ignored, male and female, rich and poor.[15]

In Ephesians 4:1-16 we find this letter's deepest insights into the basis of our unity and the goal to be achieved. The most fundamental insight, says W.A. Visser 't Hooft, is that Ephesians helps us distinguish between the *given* unity, which is inherent in the common calling, and the *ultimate* unity which we should attain. Neither the visionary definitions from apostles or ecumenical enthusiasts nor the persistent lack of unity in the church changes what we are called to be and to do. "This given unity demands realization and this realization takes the form of growth, or increase."[16]

It probably catches us by surprise that the first three verses of this Ephesians passage are a call to "lowliness and meekness, with patience, forbearing one another in love, eager to maintain the unity of the Spirit in the bond of peace" (4:2-3). Peace (*shalom*) in the Hebrew tradition means wholeness, the full harmony of persons. Yet the highway toward peace and unity is strewn with wrecked efforts and disillusioned advocates whose plans and proposals failed, not because they were inappropriate, but because people did not see or accept the fact that the route to unity begins with humility, self-emptying love, and yes, patience (literally "take pains"). We must receive God's peace and love in our hearts before we can be made one.

Verses 4-6 are a liturgical hymn or confession that rings with Paul's sevenfold unity. Hear the emphatic cadence present in the church in the late first century. These words come on the one hand as an affirmation, but on the other hand as a warning—one body, one Spirit, one hope, one Lord, one faith, one baptism, one God. But, says the writer of Ephesians, the differing gifts (*charismata*) that Christ gives are intended to manifest the unity of the church (vs. 7-10), a unity that goes beyond the church to the whole world. Markus Barth gives us a summary description of the church as described in these Ephesian verses:

> It is a humble and loving church who is responsive to her present task and eager to reach her goal. Such a church will not consider herself an empire-builder. She will not pretend that she possesses, masters, and administers the Lord and his gifts. She will be meek before the Lord and modest before unbelievers. She has a promise to trust, a way in which to go, a commitment to fulfil, and an energy given to her, which are not her own. The church is as much as, but no more than, a happy migrating people moving forward to the day of redemption. She is a hard-working community of servants who accept their call into God's witness stand for the sake of the whole creation.[17]

CHRISTIAN UNITY: MATRIX FOR MISSION

Ephesians gives us confidence—God's confidence, not our own—in the pilgrimage toward unity; but it sets before us some new, unanticipated attitudes and conditions for the road.

Finally, we turn to the high-priestly (that is, consecrated by self-giving) prayer of our Lord found in the seventeenth chapter of the Gospel according to John. This is part of the last discourse or conversation in the Johannine Gospel (chapters 13-17) where Jesus (interpreted by John) anticipates the new era which his coming death and resurrection will inaugurate. In a few hours he will be betrayed, sentenced and crucified. His work is done; his words sound like those spoken in the Kingdom. This great prayer, which William Temple called "perhaps the most sacred passage ever in the four Gospels," has been used and abused by advocates of unity and mission alike. In fact, comments Paul Minear, "aggressive evangelists and ardent ecumenists often contend with one another for the exclusive right to this text; indeed, if the bones of contention between these two were laid end to end, they would reach from Pentecost to the Parousia."[18]

The passage is not easy to read. John's language is cosmic; in this prayer he uses a literary form that says the same thing twice (compare verses 20-21 with verses 22-23).[19] His petitions to God can, however, be outlined: Christ prays (1) that his disciples (vs. 11) and those "who are to believe in me through their word" (vs. 20) may all be one; (2) that their unity will be expressed "even as thou, Father, art in me, and I in thee" (vs. 21); and (3) "so that the world may believe that thou hast sent me" (vs. 21).

Such exalted teaching is both a blessing and a bane for us. It keeps us from identifying Christ's will too easily with our ecumenical plans and institutions. At the same time, however, it judges those who stand aloof from the search for visible unity, those who plead that they fear unity or that they are tired or disillusioned. This Johannine prayer makes some striking points about the nature of Christian unity. First, the unity for which Christ prays originates in God's action. "The unity to which we are called is unity which is received and not unity which is fabricated by ourselves."[20] The fact that Jesus prays to God is evidence that the power to unite lies in God's hands. It is not in our power to make the church one; unity is God-given. But this does not mean that our role is a passive one. Participation is the proper response of faith. We are compelled to *manifest* God-given unity in word and deed. Participation can be entered into with confidence because we know that the will of the Lord of history will not ultimately be thwarted.

Second, the intensity and shape of this unity are likened to the oneness between the Father and the Son. Given John's tendency toward the mystical, some people might be tempted to misinterpret the character of the church's unity as a kind of invisible, mystical, loosely connected relationship. But the trinitarian model defines the church's unity in concrete terms, conveying distinctiveness with intimacy. Such a trinitarian relationship demands, for most students of John's Gospel, some form of organic unity, although such a premise does not buttress any particular plan of union (Church of South India or the Consultation on Church Union in the United States) or any particular concept of what unity entails (conciliar fellowship or whatever). Christian unity is a sign of the coming Kingdom and is, therefore, eschatological, pressing us from the present to the future. No higher motivation for unity can exist for Christians than that they should embody on earth the unity between God and Christ.

Third, the Johannine picture is of unity not for its own sake but for the sake of the world. Christians are sent into the world on an apostolic mission, to present to the world of unbelief and to other faiths and ideologies the same unity of love that came in Christ. In the unity of the church, the world will recognize the goal of peace and wholeness which God intends for its own destiny. Hence, unity has to be visible enough in the actual life of the church to challenge the world to believe in Jesus Christ. The high-priestly prayer further emphasizes this truth by linking church unity with the glory (Greek *doxa*) that Christ received from God: ''The glory which thou hast given me I have given to them, that they may be one even as we are one'' (vs. 22). Unity is the epiphany of God's glory made known in the incarnate Lord; glory is given to make known the church's unity. But what is this glory? It is certainly not public praises or the thrill of exercising power in the worlds of finance and politics, church or secular. Glory is suffering love whose prototype is the Cross. To glorify here means to reveal through self-denying love. Unity comes when we receive a glory that is manifested in weakness and humility, in defeat and death. ''To receive that glory means to be involved in God's work of salvation, to be on His side, to share in His victory of sin and death . . . disunity amounts to a refusal to accept the gift of the doxa.''[21] In the final analysis, unity is required if the church is to experience the ''glory as of the only Son from the Father'' (John 1:14b) and to fulfill its missionary task in and for the world.

The biblical evidence is convincingly weighty: the idea of church unity was an article of faith for the primitive apostolic community. While its members' relations one with another were not altogether harmonious, a consciousness of unity defined the reality of the church. The early Christians witnessed to Christ amid a healthy diversity of traditions, theology, forms of worship and governance, and even had animated controversies and tensions. But for them the divided state of the churches was untenable because it violated the integrity of the Church of Christ and made a mockery of Christian witness. The Bible is a call to repentance for our divisions, and a summons to manifest in Christ that unity which is a characteristic mark of his church.

4 Unity and Mission: The Heretical Dichotomy

That they may all be one ... so that the world may believe.
—John 17:21

Whenever the church accepts the fact that it is living in a missionary situation, the call to unity becomes vital. Both the Scriptures and the modern ecumenical movement speak of the indissoluble bond between unity and mission, although that bond is often one of tension. Nor is it an accident that the pioneers of the twentieth-century ecumenical movement, with their central concern for drawing the people of God together, were persons with a passion for mission and evangelism. Those whose imaginations were fired by the vision of Christ's mission to the whole world found their consciences judged by the scandal of Christian disunity. They knew that the Lord, once and for all times, gave a double-edged imperative in the gospel, having prayed "that they may all be one" and immediately adding "so that the world may believe." Those who believe the gospel know that unity is a prerequisite for truly authentic mission, and that mission forms the basis for a truly ecumenical sharing of life.

In 1915, Presbyterian missionary leader Arthur J. Brown wrote a book entitled *Unity and Missions,* which stirred the American churches.[1] His pivotal question was: "Can a divided church save the world?" His Western answer, formed out of his experience in American congregations and overseas churches, was a definite "No." The same negative answer, but delivered with more flair and passion, has come from Christians outside the West who are living their faith and witness in hostile cultures. One such classic statement was made by V.S. Azariah, the Anglican bishop of Dornakal (India) to the First World Conference on Faith and Order, held at Lausanne in 1927. At that great meeting, Bishop Azariah listened to representatives of the

43

CHRISTIAN UNITY: MATRIX FOR MISSION

Western churches discuss their differences in a manner that convinced him they were going to do little more than talk. Finally he rose and startled the conference with a piercing cry from India: "Divided Christendom is a source of weakness in the West; in non-Christian lands it is a sin and a stumbling-block. If the non-Christian world is to be won for Christ our message must be one. If our message is to be one, we must be one."[2] Even today those words should quicken our consciences.

Today we would disagree with Bishop Azariah's distinction between the Christian West and "non-Christian" countries. The so-called Christian countries have become what the French call *pays de mission,* missionary countries. Think of recent developments in the United States and Europe; Christians are being forced to realize that we all live in cultures and countries that do not really support Christian values or Christian witness. Whenever we witness to the servant Christ who loves all people and who transcends all human systems, we discover that we, too, are a church in a hostile, "non-Christian" environment. The church is everywhere in a missionary situation, far more critically than many are willing to admit; and unity is essential for our witness.

In the light of this new missionary awareness a group of American churches made a moving confession that states the dynamic relation between unity and mission:

Looking at us, the world is unimpressed by our claim to love one another, when it sees how we are fractured and divided by our lesser loyalties. Our protestations that Christ has broken down the walls between men are belied by the barriers we erect to cut off even Christians from one another. We act as if the Church were ours, forgetting that he "is able from these stones to raise up children to Abraham" (Matthew 3:9 RSV). Many things which Christ counted essential tend to become non-essential in our eyes; and things which he views as non-essential we often treat as essential. Even though we all affirm the same basic confession and are bound by common loyalty to the one Lord, we do not allow his demands to yoke us together in common tasks nor his promises to draw us together as pilgrims to the same City. Bound by the same Scripture, we do not listen together to its judgment or together receive its grace. Baptized into the dying and rising of Christ, we allow neither ourselves nor others to grasp the full power of that baptism. We join him at his Table, receiving his body and blood, but we are not thereby impelled to sorrow over our divisions nor led to heal them. Our churches often appear to the world not as servants of the servant Christ but as affluent, self-perpetuating

44

enterprises competing with one another. These things the world sees, and is dismayed and alienated by them, alienated from God and from us.[3]

"These things" — our lesser loyalties, our assumption that the church belongs to us, our divided confessions of the one Lord, our abuse of the sacraments given to reconcile and send forth, our acceptance of the status of competitors rather than servants of our common Lord—are acts of disobedience that cause disbelief in the world. "These things," which signal disunity in the church, flagrantly deny something essential for Christian mission. Thirty years after it was spoken, the pronouncement of a world missionary conference still rings true: "Division in the Church distorts its witness, frustrates its mission, and contradicts its own nature. If the Church is to demonstrate the Gospel in its *life* as well as in its preaching, it must manifest to the world the power of God to break down all barriers and to establish the Church's unity in Christ. *Christ is not divided.*"[4] The same judgment is declared by Vatican Council II: Disunity "openly contradicts the will of Christ, provides a stumbling block to the world, and inflicts damage on the most holy cause of proclaiming the good news to every creature" *(Decree on Ecumenism,* section 1). "Division among Christians . . . blocks the way to the faith for many. Hence, by the same mandate which makes missions necessary, all the baptized are called to be gathered into one flock, and thus to be able to bear unanimous witness before the nations to Christ their Lord" *(Decree on the Missionary Activity of the Church,* section 6).

These truths have frequently become platitudes to which we give mere lip service in speeches and books. Nevertheless, the issue will not rest. Something far more profound is at stake. The main reason mission and evangelism are hindered by disunity is not that unity would increase efficiency and cooperation—rather, it is that when they are divided, the churches' character betrays their witness. The herald denies in its own life the very message it is assigned to proclaim; the specially-ordained sign no longer incarnates the redeeming salvation of the Giver.

The church's calling to unity is a calling in mission. This truth must, however, be translated into the realities of today's world. Since today the words *unity* and *mission* are under a cloud, we need to do some probing of both. In Chapter 7 we shall speak about the shape of unity, but in this chapter we shall discuss the meaning of mission, a topic of no small disagreement among those who care. Does *mission* differ from *evangelism*? What is meant by the proclamation of the Word as an event that leads individuals to faith and repentance? What is implied when we speak of transforming the patterns of society so that human institutions and structures more nearly convey respect and freedom? How are mission and evangelism related to the spiritual issues of hunger, poverty, injustice and war? Can mission be directed to human welfare as well as human salvation; and if so, what is the difference between the two? These are some of the questions under debate, and good, caring Christians can be found on either side of the debate.

Such questions need not convey alternatives, although a number of churches are embroiled in controversy over them. Polarization over these questions is in one sense frightening, especially when one realizes it could lead to new divisions within the churches. But in another sense, this debate can aid the churches in the search for a truth that will not let us forget that in our differences, even on such sacred matters, we belong together. At this point I shall not choose sides in the current debate about mission. Rather, I shall make my own apologia — my own confession — of the meaning of mission and evangelism and their relation to unity. I shall stress four dimensions that come, I believe, from the gospel — proclamation, presence, service and Eucharist.

MISSION AND EVANGELISM AS PROCLAMATION

The mission of the church is, first, to proclaim the Word of God to the whole world. Mission means telling all people the good news that Christ has reconciled the world to God. It means bringing the encouraging word that amidst sin and shame God entered history in the person of Jesus Christ to redeem humanity. It means declaring the great things God has done and is doing for people: breaking the chains of our bondage to sin and the powers of the earth; initiating us into a new and victorious life that includes struggle but is a foretaste of the coming Kingdom; giving us a new and living hope. Mission is proclaiming in word and deed this *message*.

The New Testament uses three words to describe proclamation: *katagellein, kerrussein* and *euangelizesthai. Katagellein* means to announce, but the nuance is that the announcement is made with authority. In ancient Greece the word was used to announce a festival, to proclaim the accession of a new emperor to the throne or to announce a declaration of war. In the Acts of the Apostles it is used a number of times, for example, for the prophets who *proclaimed* the coming of Christ (Acts 3:24) and for Paul's instruction to Barnabas that they again visit "every city where we *proclaimed* the word of the Lord, and see how they are" (Acts 15:36).

Kerrussein means to herald, to make a dramatic declaration in an atmosphere of importance and wonder. The messenger is a representative of the king. Among the Greeks it was a proclamation, a television newsflash if you please, made in broad daylight with a fanfare of trumpets and addressed to all the people because it was from the king. In the New Testament this word is used to tell of the coming of God's kingdom. For example, Mark writes: "Jesus came into Galilee, *preaching* the gospel of God, and saying, 'The time is fulfilled, and the kingdom of God is at hand; repent, and believe in the gospel' " (Mark 1:14-15).

Euangelizesthai means to announce good news, glad tidings — usually news that people have not heard or expected. In Greek history the evangelist was the one who announced a major event—a victory, the beginning of the games or some other key moment in the life of the empire. Old Testament writers use this term to tell the good news of God's decisive and saving actions on behalf of Israel, delivering it from its enemies and its own sins. In the New Testament Peter uses the term in his famous sermon about God showing no partiality: "You know the word which he sent to Israel, preaching good news of peace by Jesus Christ (he is Lord of all), the word which was *proclaimed* throughout all Judea" (Acts 10:36-37).

As we learn from these early Christian usages, the missionary proclamation is "nothing apologetic, nothing diffident, nothing clouded with doubts and misted with uncertainties."[5] On the other hand, it is never arrogant, blaring or self-righteous preaching. It is simply the proclamation, humble but with authority, of Christ as Lord. A decade ago Peter Berger, the sociologist of religion, chided the American churches for a demoralized condition marked most by "a failure of nerve." In the changing world of the 1960s, many church people became meek and short-sighted "prophets of relevance" who could be recognized by their hesitancy and caution rather than by their commitment to the faith "once and for all delivered to the saints." The churches, he felt, had diluted their message and eclipsed their fundamental mission. As an antidote Berger called upon the churches to adopt a "stance of authority," that is, to move from uncertain silence to faith-proclamation, from a loss of nerve to a bold telling of the story of faith. "Ages of faith are not marked by dialogue but by proclamation."[6] We may not accept his negative reference to dialogue, but Berger's call to authoritative proclamation identifies an essential part of Christian witness. We should not forget Bonhoeffer's commentary on the Confessing Church in Germany toward the close of World War II. This church, he said, "has only fought for her self-preservation as if she were an end in herself, and thereby has lost her authority to proclaim the reconciling and redemptive word for [hu]mankind and the world."[7]

An important issue must be faced, however: Christian proclamation is not propaganda. Witness in the deepest sense means the denial of all propaganda. Selling a new missionary strategy, offering a gimmick for stewardship or relief funds, pushing the latest ideology, identifying a program with a star personality—such techniques often characterize a propaganda campaign rather than mission for Christ's service. This recurring sin plagues electronic evangelists, mission boards, charitable organizations, local pastors and stewardship committees alike.

Mission and evangelism present Jesus Christ, the risen Lord, as the hope of the world. "For what we preach is not ourselves," said the apostle Paul. "Ourselves" can mean our favorite mission program, our denomination's work presented in global splendor, our people on the mission frontiers. Instead, says Paul, we proclaim "Jesus Christ as Lord, with ourselves as your servants for Jesus' sake" (2 Cor. 4:5). That is proclamation with authority that shines through in both content and style. Propaganda, by contrast, is ego-serving; it exalts me, my church, my world view, my values. The mission theologian Hans Hoekendijk distinguished propaganda this way: "Propaganda's essential character is a lack of expectant hope and an absence of due humility. The propagandist has to impose himself. He has to resort to himself, to his work. . . . In short, the propagandist tries to make exact copies of himself."[8]

Those engaged in propaganda, as distinct from proclamation, become voices of human ideology. They attract people to a certain system of ideas and values. The test of faith becomes loyalty to a particular theology or confessional stance, a certain project or a certain institution. The gospel momentarily becomes captive to a personality, a political system, a culture or a doctrine. Let us candidly confess: whether to proclaim Christ or to propagandize an ideology is a perennial dilemma facing the church in any age, but it especially tempts this generation. We can be saved from a tragic mistake if we are clear that proclamation bears witness to a saving person, Jesus Christ, and points to a redemptive event that gathers all women and men into relation with him. This person and event sum up the meaning of our existence.

Clearly, a true mission always proclaims unity because its message transcends the boundaries of institutions and traditions that divide; likewise in this proclamation we are inevitably pointed to the source of our oneness, the mission of the people of God. In this sense unity makes our mission more authentic since Christians are often tempted to proclaim the gospel of Christ in the name of a particular theology or institution.

MISSION AND EVANGELISM AS PRESENCE

There can be no proclamation without presence, by which we mean the adventure of going to live with others in the world in the name of Christ. The meaning of Christian presence can be seen in Charles de Foucauld, a Roman Catholic missionary, who dedicated his life to serving the poor of the Muslim world, particularly the Touareg peoples of the Sahara desert. He lived twelve years among them with few rewards except pain and hardship. In the end (1916) he was murdered by the people whom he came to serve. But through his life and death, he ignited the hearts of millions of people and he left, as not the least of his legacies, the order of the Little Brothers of Jesus. A passage from an inspiring biography of Father de Foucauld reveals his spirit:

> The deep charity which marked Charles de Foucauld's approach to Islam is the key to the presentation of the Christian character. We must go forward with a profound respect for all men created by God in His image. With this respect there must be linked a sense of brotherhood and a recognition of the integrity of those with whom we deal. If we can *show in our lives the simplicity of the Christian character* we cannot fail to begin to break down the effect of the centuries of prejudice which have separated Islam from the Catholic religion.[9]

I never fully understood the power of such a "simplicity of the Christian character" until I became friendly with a United Presbyterian fraternal worker in Egypt. His was a story—unsuccessful by all church growth manual standards — of twenty years of Christian witness in an Islamic society. My Presbyterian friend, Father de Foucauld and countless others radiate a spirit that communicates humility and faith. This spirit can penetrate the barriers that separate Christians from persons of other living faiths, Christians from agnostics, Christians from one another. The life of Charles de Foucauld sums up this concept of mission and evangelism: "His vocation was one of being *present* amongst people, with a presence willed and intended as a witness of the love of Christ."[10]

The World Student Christian Federation (WSCF) in its mission to the academic world also speaks of presence. For these students the word *presence* describes "the adventure of being there in the name of Christ." This presence is achieved "often anonymously, listening before speaking, hoping that men [and women] will recognize Jesus for what he is and stay where they are, involved in the fierce fight against all that dehumanizes, ready to act against demonic powers, to identify with the outcast, merciless in ridiculing modern idols and new myths."[11] Some conservative-evangelical missiologists, like Donald McGavran, have pounced on this WSCF paper as a commentary on an uncertainty of faith, especially in its reference to "listening." But that is to miss the point. A witnessing presence is not one of total silence. Rather, the evangelistic posture includes "listening before we speak," and recognizing that sometimes the most powerful witness to Christ is made incognito, without recognition of the evangelist. Presence conveys the love of Christ through one's lifestyle as well as through one's spoken words.

Ironically, such presence usually comes before any missionary activity is effective. In his book *Missions in a Time of Testing,* Ronald K. Orchard, a former executive of the World Council of Churches' (WCC) Commission on World Mission and Evangelism, presses the point:

> The first result of commitment to Jesus Christ is to receive the new quality of life that is His gift, and to live it. In that sense, *being* is prior to *doing* in the Christian life. Mission is presence before it is action— the presence in any human situation of those who live by the new life in Christ and so are by their very presence witnesses to the new action. . . . Mission is the passivity of being at God's disposal before it is the activity of any deliberate act of witness.[12]

It is important that we who are conditioned to think in terms of instant action hear Orchard correctly. He is not calling for a do-nothing policy in face of the crises where courageous mission is required. He takes mission seriously, saying that it is revealed in the lives of those who are true servants of Christ in the world. "Because they knew how to live 'being present' with God, they were able to 'be present' quite spontaneously with people of every kind and in every circumstance," says Max Warren.[13] The quality of the life we live among others is the most dramatic credential of our witness.

Mission as presence is a call to action in the sense that it is a call not just to be *in* the world but to struggle with and *for* the world. It means being present with God in the world through solidarity with God's suffering and rejected children. In mission, Christians are asked to stand with those who declare the gospel in their suffering, to accompany them in their confrontation with the violent powers and principalities of injustice, as well as in their fight with the silent powers and principalities of hunger and illiteracy. Mission as presence requires us to share their wretchedness and horror. This calling inevitably means that there is a divine connection between mission and politics, between evangelism and suffering witness, between the proclamation of the gospel of Jesus Christ and participation in human liberation. Such an active presence is essential if the other efforts we make in proclamation and compassion are to be effective. The wretched of the earth hear and receive Christ's love through acts of solidarity.

An illustration can be seen in the most controversial ecumenical program in many years, the WCC's Program to Combat Racism (PCR). The PCR was set up to help the churches achieve greater understanding of, and more effective means for overcoming, the awful affliction of racial prejudice. But from the beginning the program has been a focus of debate. Many representatives at the WCC's Nairobi Assembly (1975) were uncertain about the renewal of the PCR's initial mandate. In the midst of this skepticism and subdued anger, a bold statement of support was offered by Burgess Carr, then general secretary of the All-Africa Conference of Churches. "Whatever else you may think of this program of the WCC, it is a ray of hope for the oppressed and down-trodden people of Africa. It has caused many Africans to take seriously the claim of Jesus Christ upon their lives and the life of their nation."[14]

An equally penetrating word came in relation to the PCR's $85,000 grant on August 10, 1978 to the Patriotic Liberation Front (PLF) in Zimbabwe. At the time the PLF was one of the three freedom movements working for the independence of Zimbabwe/ Rhodesia from white domination; the leader of this movement, Robert Mugabe, has since become prime minister of the elected government. Reports of the WCC grant were terribly distorted by the Western press and media. The WCC was portrayed as supporting violence, giving money to buy "guns for guerrillas," when in reality the money was for humanitarian needs, as are all PCR grants. This particular grant bought food and medicine, and set up a school and a clinic to be used by the wives and children of the freedom fighters who were in dire need in jungle camps in neighboring Mozambique.

Even now, years later, little of the true story has replaced the distortions that hit the newspapers. Many Christians in North America and Europe are still enraged by what they believe was an unwarranted meddling in politics. Yet my deepest memory of those hot days is of a public meeting in Indianapolis in 1979 when I listened to an address by the Honourable Garfield Todd, a former Disciples missionary to Rhodesia who later served that country as prime minister. After Dr. Todd spoke, there was a barrage of questions about Zimbabwe and its future. But the burning question was put by a young pastor who came to the meeting scarred from trying to interpret the WCC grant to his hostile, misinformed congregation. "Sir," he asked, "what do you think about the WCC's grant?" In an unwavering voice this great Christian leader replied: "Because of that grant Christ again walks through the villages of Zimbabwe/Rhodesia." It is not enough to voice abstract support for those who suffer. We must seek to be present with them.

In the last analysis, mission and evangelism as presence in human struggles are a witness to our incarnate Lord. In this sense witness means living out our Christology. "The Word became flesh and dwelt among us, full of grace and truth" (John 1:14a) is more than a memory verse for children. It is a mandate for incarnational evangelism. What is at stake is not just the future of a particular mission style or project, but the integrity of the church's life and the credibility of our witness to Christ as Lord of all.

The ecumenical impact of this presence is clear. Divisions undermine Christian presence. Unity is essential in order for the love of the one Lord to radiate from our presence in the world.

MISSION AND EVANGELISM AS SERVICE

Service is at the heart of Christ's ministry, as defined in the verse: "I am among you as one who serves" (Luke 22:27). The Greek word for service is *diakonia,* literally "table service," a role which in Jesus' day was considered undignified and demeaning. Yet Jesus' whole life ultimately dignified such a role — by humbling himself, washing the feet of the disciples, healing, advocating the needs of the poor, the sick, the imprisoned, the homeless. His disciples are expected to do the same: we are called to serve with the Servant Lord. *Diakonia* means helping out, bearing burdens for someone else as an act of mutual fellowship.

Christian witness, from the time of the first apostles, has included acts of *diakonia*, particularly to "the least of these." Paul's collection for the impoverished church at Jerusalem, sometimes referred to as the first program of interchurch aid, was a prime deed of Christian service. In his second letter to the Corinthians, he appeals to them to take part in "the *relief* of the saints" (2 Cor. 8:4), "the *offering* for the saints" (9:1), and "this *service*" (9:12). In each case he uses the same word, *diakonia*. Paul believes the offering will demonstrate two things. First, it will make clear God's acceptance of both the Gentiles and the Jews. Second, it will be an act of love that will manifest the unity of the church. Critical tensions may have existed between the Gentile congregations (built by Paul) and the church in Jerusalem, but they belonged to the one body of Christ. This means that nothing less than a ministry of service and relief is required of Christians because we follow a servant Lord and because, in Christ's body, "If one member suffers, all suffer together" (1 Cor. 12:26).

In this tradition of Christian *diakonia*, the churches in the ecumenical movement have developed jointly a program of service to human need. Two important symbols of this work at the national and international level are Church World Service (CWS), a division of the National Council of the Churches of Christ in the U.S.A., and the WCC's Commission on Inter-church Aid, Refugee and World Service (CICARWS, pronounced see-car-wis). Both are channels of compassion and service through which millions of dollars in food, medicine and development aid are delivered each year. The money and resources deployed in this part of the ecumenical movement are staggering and humbling. Undoubtedly this is the most impressive part of the ministry of the church in our time.[15]

Interchurch aid in its ecumenical form developed immediately after World War II. When the war in Europe ended in 1945, Christian leaders recognized a responsibility for the rehabilitation and relief of those who had suffered. Church buildings destroyed by war had to be rebuilt. More important, lives and hopes that had been dashed by this global disaster had to be reclaimed. A program of interchurch aid was set in motion, through the generosity of the North American, Swiss and Swedish churches, "to rebuild the whole life of the fellowship of churches."[16] Assistance was given to reconstitute devastated orphanages, hospitals, schools and homes for the aged. Blankets, food, clothing, medicines and other symbols of life were delivered. Spiritual and material care was given to twelve million "displaced persons" or refugees. Undernourished pastors and their families, terribly weakened emotionally and physically, were renewed for future ministry. Funds and fraternal workers were made available to help the churches resume such tasks as evangelism and Christian education. All these expressions of service became a modern drama of Christian love in action. ''Men and women experienced the reality of the life of the Church of Jesus Christ through the acts of Christian fellowship.''[17]

From those beginnings this Christian *diakonia* became a permanent and superlative part of the ecumenical movement. It is instructive, however, to note changing requirements of service brought about by changes in the world. A review of these changes may provide insights into the meaning of Christian service.

Two signs of a new meaning of *diakonia* were articulated at the Evanston Assembly (1954) of the WCC: the places of interchurch aid were extended beyond Europe to include the churches of Asia, Africa and Latin America; and the one-sided concept of aid was enlarged to become ''mutual aid,'' that is, aid whereby all churches give and receive.

The New Delhi Assembly (1961) brought even more radical developments in the face of new factors confronting the churches and the world. Political and economic crises had begun to create a new generation of refugees and migrants; the gap between developed and less-developed nations was widening; the problems of new, emerging nations and the population explosion seared the consciences of Christians. These challenges could not be met by the traditional church-to-church approach to interchurch aid; the needs of peoples, irrespective of their church affiliation, became paramount. Thus, in addition to relief work and dealing with emergencies created by natural and social disasters, the task became ''to express the ecumenical *solidarity* of the churches through mutual aid in order to strengthen them in their life and mission and especially in their service (*diakonia*) to the world around them.''

The shift was significant. From a church-to-church service there emerged a clear perspective of ''a worldwide *diakonia*'' that helps meet the needs of humanity regardless of creed, caste, race, nationality or politics. Though the name stayed the same, the function changed from interchurch aid to interhuman aid. Christian service came to mean helping churches to be an effective presence in societies where nation building, family development, feeding the hungry, human rights and other such issues dominated their destiny.

Two further emphases arose at the Uppsala Assembly (1968) which extended the churches' task. Interchurch aid was acknowledged to involve *justice* and *development*. In an international society where social and political injustices are the plight of millions, relief and rehabilitation alone are an inadequate expression of Christian *diakonia*. "All our work of compassion must be done in the context of a just solution."[18] In a world where hunger, unemployment and poverty increase their ugly stranglehold on millions upon millions, shipments of rice and wheat alone will not suffice as a caring response. The churches now felt called to strike at the root causes of human suffering by giving funds, technology and political commitments in order to help persons be free, self-reliant and able to realize their God-given potential. Pope Paul VI spoke in a similar vein in his important encyclical on world development and aid to the Third World, *Populorum Progressio* (1967). "The new name for peace is development," he said, in a plea to all nations and churches. Just as peace cannot be limited to the absence of war, so service cannot be limited to cooperation in charitable acts.

> Peace is something that is built day after day, in the pursuit of an order intended by God, which implies a more perfect form of justice among men [and women]. . . . To wage war on misery and to struggle against injustice is to promote . . . the common good of all humanity. (paragraph 76)

Finally, a discussion of *diakonia* in the church must take account of the relation of service to evangelism and of service to Christian unity. Is service an instrument of evangelism? Do we weigh its importance by the number of persons it leads to accept the gospel? Many people in the developing countries suspect that Christian service has the ulterior motive of "winning souls"; the price of food, they assume, is conversion. Such views are hardly surprising when churches who offer partnership in service look on quietly as the governments of their countries use food and aid as bribes in world politics. True *diakonia* has no motive other than to be "a response to the costly love of God for the whole world."[19] There are no conditions which the receiver must fulfill—gratitude, conversion or whatever. Service in the name of Christ is "service without calculation" (Visser 't Hooft), because the recipients are among those for whom Christ died.

Does service unite or divide? This question is crucial for the emerging structures and strategies of interchurch aid. And as with many such questions, the working answer is "Both." In some places structures of Christian aid preserve church division. For example, years ago the Church of South India and the Lutherans in India resolved their theological differences and publicized their doctrinal consensus. But twenty years later these two churches remain divided because the Lutherans in South India fear that if they become part of a united church their contributions from Lutheran churches in other parts of the world will be reduced or eliminated. The Church of Christ in Zaire faces the same tensions. Its growth toward fuller unity is hampered by the desire of Presbyterians and Methodists and others within this united church to keep their denominational dollars coming directly to them. We cannot sidestep the fact: service and mission funds *can* divide churches when they are given exclusively through denominational channels, or when they preserve patterns of dependency, or when they keep the centers of power and influence primarily in the wealthy Western churches or ecumenical agencies. Even Christian service organizations can contribute to division when they become enmeshed in a bureaucracy dedicated to its own self-preservation. This is to offer aid without true *diakonia*. When Christian humility is replaced by the lust for power—a drive to control or patronize—then service programs will divide. The insight of Professor Nikos Nissiotis, a leading Orthodox theologian from Athens, is very important here: the root of division and schism in the church, past and present, lies in "the lack of care of local churches for one another, the absence of *diakonia* between them."[20]

Fortunately, interchurch aid is also a sign of the growing unity of the church. As the churches respond to earthquakes in Guatemala, Italy or Greece, as they respond to drought and hunger in the Sahel or Cambodia, as they relocate refugees from Vietnam or Palestine, as they underwrite fish hatcheries in Indonesia, secure jobs for bakers in Chile, train unemployed handicapped fathers in Sri Lanka, their *diakonia* becomes a testimony to our real unity in Christ. Service can be a mighty force in the growth of Christian unity. The needs of the world can push the churches beyond their provincial boundaries. This does not happen easily or automatically; it can only happen if our service is designed and programmed in such a way as to draw us together to be servants of the reconciling Christ. The WCC's Commission on Inter-church Aid, Refugee and World Service realizes what is at stake:

> The quality of our service can be enriched by the depth of our unity or limited by our divisions. Unity is expressed in service, deepened by service and tested by service. Our growth in unity is challenged and renewed by the tensions we experience as we seek the wholeness of the Church and the wholeness of humankind.[21]

Paul said it first: "All this is from God, who through Christ reconciled us to himself and gave us the ministry [*diakonia*] of reconciliation" (2 Cor. 5:18).

MISSION AND EVANGELISM AS EUCHARIST

The idea of mission and evangelism as Eucharist may seem strange to some readers, but clearly many Christians now see a relationship between mission and the worshiping community, especially in the Lord's Supper. In one sense it seems incredible that churches can separate their understanding of mission from the sacraments. Yet one need only survey the sacramental teachings of churches or the reports of mission agencies in the churches to see how often mission is considered outside the eucharistic context. When this happens both mission and the sacraments are disfigured. The sacraments become merely ecclesiastical rituals for the care of those who "come to church," meaning those who come to the building where the congregation regularly gathers. Baptism and the Lord's Supper become individualistic, other-worldly and inward-looking instead of opening Christians to the world. Separated from the sacraments, mission becomes merely a humanitarian program, "doing good for others," practicing a solidarity without a sense of the presence of Christ to transform and change; it ceases to point to the Kingdom of God.

During the 1966 Conference on Church and Society, a Swiss newspaper reporter asked Eugene Carson Blake, an American who had recently been elected the second general secretary of the WCC, how the church could contribute to the creative transformation of society. His answer probably was not what the press expected from a courageous prophet of ecumenism who had walked in protest marches for racial justice, been a cofounder of Bread for the World and preached the dramatic sermon that launched the Consultation on Church Union. This man, identified with so many causes where faith required that one's reputation be put on the line, said the transforming power of the church is sustained

> above all by its regular acts of worship offered to God. According to our several traditions we read the Bible; we pray, we give thanks, we make petitions and we intercede; we administer the sacraments; and we sing to the glory of God. . . . I am taking the opportunity to refer to this because certain of us, in our great desire to improve upon the past, forget the central importance for the Church of the offering of worship

CHRISTIAN UNITY: MATRIX FOR MISSION

to God. Unless I believed this I would long ago have joined my efforts
to some other institution which may be more effective in achieving
social change.[22]

The weakness of any practice that polarizes mission and sacramental worship is also observed by Emilio Castro, director of the
WCC's Commission on World Mission and Evangelism:

In the hard Latin American situation, face to face with oppression, it is
important for those who fight for the cause of justice to be rooted in a
worshipping community. They need the personal experience with the
God who liberates, to understand that even their historical failures are
not the final word, but they are enrolled in the service of God who
knows the secret of history and knows how to use even failures to carry
history to its goal.[23]

From two continents comes the truth I am trying to establish: a
missionary presence is the fruit of participation in the Lord's Supper.
"Every eucharistic gathering is therefore an act of witness, which is a
part of mission."[24] The communion table is the matrix of mission,
the place where church and world intersect in the presence of Christ,
the place from which Christians are sent forth to serve and to love.

The integral link between mission and the Lord's Supper sets
before us two startling reminders. First, Christian mission can be
done only at great cost to those who accept the task. This was true of
Christ's ministry and mission, fulfilled at the cost of the cross. His
broken body and shed blood represent for us the price tag of obedience to God's redeeming and liberating purposes. Here the biblical
word *martus,* one of the Greek words for *witness* from which the
English word *martyr* is derived, illustrates the point. In the New
Testament a martyr is one who testifies to the central facts about the
life, death and Resurrection of Jesus of Nazareth. But this witness
inevitably meets open opposition, and draws the martyr into conflict
with others in the world. Although mission always has a cost, we
unduly limit the meaning of *martyr* when we use it only for those who
are killed because of their Christian faith. A martyr is a person who,
often in the ordinary surroundings of the home or working place, pays
the price for his or her witness.

Second, when mission and the Lord's Supper are viewed together,
the divisions of the churches at the table become even more ridiculous
and sad. Is it not incredible in this advanced era of the ecumenical
movement that church practices and rules still do not regularly en-
courage (among Protestants) or permit (among Orthodox, Roman

58

Catholic) the common celebration of the Eucharist? My point is not a tacit call for irresponsible action. We must respect the problems that define this disgraceful division. We cannot ignore conflicting patterns of ministry, different eucharistic teachings and practices, differing doctrines of Christ's presence and sacrifice, or debates over whether sharing the Lord's Supper is a means toward visible unity in Christ or the ultimate expression of this unity. But respect for these problems, upon which theologians are making significant progress, does not mean acquiescence in the condition of brokenness.

> It is Christ, present in the Eucharist, who invites all Christians to his table; this direct invitation of Christ cannot be thwarted by ecclesiastical discipline. In the communion at the holy table, divided Christians are committed in a decisive way to make manifest their total, visible and organic unity.[25]

Eucharistic divisions undoubtedly frustrate the mission of the church in the world. The needs of a suffering world, therefore, call us to share the one bread and the one cup of the Lord.

Proclamation, presence, service and eucharistic sharing are four characteristics of a truly missionary life. These are the apostolic functions of those whom Christ sends to the ends of the earth to be witnesses of his words and deeds. These are the marks of the church which in Christ's name lives for others and so manifests the fullness of God's love spread throughout the whole world.

5 The Unity of the Church and the Reconciliation of the Human Family

A decade or so ago, just as the ecumenical movement reached a period of major achievement, the world changed. Or so it seemed to many who were working for church unity. The churches found themselves confronting a terrifying array of problems that divided humanity: war in Southeast Asia and the Middle East, racial conflict in North America and Africa, massive poverty and starvation in the Third World, the ominous threat of nuclear catastrophe, the pervasive denial of human rights. Equally important, the churches found that these problems could not be dealt with as they had been in the past. The world seemed considerably smaller. Poverty in India could no longer be overlooked in the United States. Europe could no longer ignore the increasingly articulate voices calling for change in Africa and Latin America. In the face of these changes in the world it became apparent that our approach to unifying the church also had to be refocused. Today we can see more clearly that church unity has to be pursued within the context of the larger search for the unity of humankind.

The problems, of course, are not totally new, nor is the ecumenical movement's awareness of them. The great early ecumenists had all been centrally concerned with the mission of the church (see Chapter 4). Church unity, they argued, is a prerequisite for effective mission to the world with its divisions of poverty, race, class and national interest. The first step must be a reconciled church that will serve as a sign to a broken humanity.

Our new realization of this fact takes two forms. First, we have begun to see that the divisions of the world are themselves the primary obstacles to church union. Traditional divisions among Roman Catholics, Methodists, Disciples, Lutherans, Baptists, Presbyterians, television evangelists and so on are far from being overcome. But the most traumatic divisions even within the church itself are between rich and poor, between women and men, between black and white, between differing ideologies, between those who demand that the church take a stand against social injustice and those who think the church should remain "above politics." These, we now see, are decisive walls of hostility that keep us apart.

The second and more positive realization has been that talk of church unity is shallow unless it is seen in the context of the search for a renewed and reconciled human community. The search for a theological consensus of faith, ministry and sacraments remains an indispensable part of ecumenical work, but it is far from being the whole picture. To speak of a fellowship in the one faith that is divorced from the realities of oppression and conflict in the world is to resign the church and the ecumenical movement to irrelevance. But to confront world issues of nuclear war and liberation without one church, which is a sign of the sacramental presence of Jesus Christ, is to ignore the distinctive Christian witness for human renewal. In our discussion of the scriptural basis of unity (Chapter 3), we saw that the context for Christ's prayer that his followers be one is the ultimate reconciliation of all humanity with God. Unless the church takes this fundamental human brokenness as its starting point, its search for unity will be tragically incomplete. Our divisions, we now realize, are deeper than we had imagined, but our vision of unity in Christ is also grander than we had allowed ourselves to dream.

Why did this new awareness dawn when it did? One reason is certainly that the human potential for destruction is greater than ever before. The church has always had war and poverty to confront, but never before could human divisions result in total annihilation. At the same time the world is experiencing a new interdependence. To say that humankind is more united than in the past may be an overstatement, but there is no doubt that technological advances have dramatically multiplied our opportunities for human encounter and have confronted humanity with a common set of social and political problems. The Western churches can no longer escape involvement in the global conflicts caused by race, politics and wealth.

Perhaps the most overlooked reason for this new awareness of the unity of the church in relation to the unity of humankind is that theologians from developing countries have become far more articulate in expressing the experience of their churches—an experience in which questions of sacrament and polity are often subordinated to the struggle against oppression and poverty. I remember vividly how the unity of the church in the midst of the unity of humankind was brought home to me by the Argentine theologian José Miguez-Bonino in 1973 at an ecumenical conference in Salamanca, Spain.[1] We had come to discuss "concepts of unity and models of union." Some of us read papers from North American and European perspectives on the problems that thwarted unity. Dr. Miguez shocked us with an analysis quite different from—and indeed, very disturbing to —most of our strategies.

The Latin American approach to unity, he said, locates the problem of division and unity not in the historical differences between denominations or confessions, but in the concrete situation "as it presents itself for those of us who strive to become aware of what it means to be God's people in the time of suffering and hope in which our people are living." The existence of different denominations is not the scandal of the church today, he claimed; competition among the churches, at least among the major confessions, has become minimal in Latin America. "There are no great and public breaches of courtesy and even of fellowship. For the great public, the peaceful coexistence and eventual union of the churches is already taken for granted." And even when denominational differences are invoked to justify separate churches, this is often a smokescreen obscuring other, more divisive, issues. For example, certain denominations in Latin America are proliberation while others are conservative and supportive of the status quo. The real scandal, Miguez declared, is the "conflicting and mutually exclusive understandings of what it means to be Christian in Latin America in the last third of the twentieth century."[2] What divides the churches is not confessional conflict, but the definition of what it means to be the church in mission.

> In other words, towards the end of the twentieth century we are caught in the din and confusion of the struggle for a new organization of human life and society. The churches, sociologically and ideologically shaped, united and divided by previous systems, are also in crisis as new forms of articulation of Christian life, of the Christian message, of theology and organization begin to emerge.[3]

The quest for Christian unity is more than an abstract exercise, conditioned only by the lines of division of a previous era and of a particular cultural milieu. The new quest offers a reborn relevance if the churches have the courage to pursue it. "For us," he concluded, "the search for unity is the struggle for the Church as it strives to take shape in the quest for a new kind of human life in a new society."[4]

I do not agree with Dr. Miguez on every point. He fails, it seems to me, to appreciate the true divisiveness among denominations in the West and he judges church unions and councils of churches too rigidly, giving them little credit for renewing themselves and dealing with the same divisive human issues he and others identify. But it is vitally important that we listen to his voice because it proclaims the new awareness about unity. The brokenness of humankind and the human struggle for renewed and reconciled community have immense implications for our vision of unity in Christ. At stake is a fundamental definition of Christian fellowship and witness, a definition that touches the very essence of the church.

NEW CHURCH-DIVIDING ISSUES

To understand more deeply the shift in ecumenical focus, we must now consider the unity of the church in relation to some of the new church-dividing issues, in the United States and Canada as well as in Latin America, Asia, Africa and the Pacific Islands. Any number of crisis concerns could fall under our surveillance, but we shall concentrate on five. Anyone who is realistically in touch with the search for Christian unity these days knows that God has these heart-rending issues on the agenda of such ecumenical bodies as the World Council of Churches, national councils of churches and the Consultation on Church Union in the United States. They are the faith issues with which congregations and denominational plenary bodies are struggling. Taken together they give us a fuller understanding of the shape and context for our unity in Christ.

Church Unity and the Struggle for Justice
The struggle for justice is the story of both the Bible and the daily newspaper. Today there is a new awareness of injustices around the globe, taking particular and horrible form in different countries. The denial of human rights, oppressive economic structures that keep some people poor and others rich, brutality against those who disagree with their governments, political tensions of all sorts—these become daily headlines about people forced to live without dignity and humaneness, without power to influence their own lives. In these particular situations Christians are called to know and proclaim God's purpose of justice in history and in the world of politics and economics. As the World Conference on Mission and Evangelism at Melbourne (1980) reminded us:

CHRISTIAN UNITY: MATRIX FOR MISSION

> There is a need for the churches to awaken to their prophetic task in the many struggles—to say ''yes'' to that which conforms to the Kingdom of God as revealed to humankind in the life of Jesus Christ, and say ''no'' to that which distorts the dignity and the freedom of human beings and all that is alive.[5]

In the face of this task the churches are tempted by two alternatives. They are, first, tempted to remain silent in order to preserve a false unity, or to avoid creating controversy within institutions and plenary bodies. They are tempted, second, to invite division by a self-righteous spirit that quickly chooses for or against a specific issue. Neither of these paths leads to genuine ecumenism. When justice is at stake God requires far more struggling from the faithful.

The struggle for wholeness is with the principalities and powers of this world, with those who so control the world that they win big while others lose. Such ecumenical witness is seen in the current generation of martyrs for whom the liberation of their people is more sacred than their own lives. One of the patron saints among them is the martyred Roman Catholic archbishop, Oscar Arnulfo Romero, born in 1917 in the *barrios* (slum dwellings) of El Salvador. After studies in his own country and in Rome, he was ordained a priest in 1942 and became a bishop in 1970. In 1977 he was made Archbishop of San Salvador.

This shy yet jovial man became Latin America's most respected voice against violence and social injustice. In his tormented and oppressed country of El Salvador, where a dictatorial government and miserable poverty join hands to visit injustices and inhuman acts upon the people, Romero became a symbol of change and hope. His weekly sermons at the cathedral were dramatic announcements of God's good news, opposing specific injustices and oppression caused by the Salvadorian junta. ''The mission of the Church,'' he preached, ''is to denounce violence, to announce justice and peace, to preach love. Such acts not only belong to the Church's most intimate nature but are an essential contribution for the overcoming of violence and injustice in El Salvador.'' Later, the day before his assassination, the archbishop appealed to the police and national guard to stop participating in the terrorizing and murder of their own people — poor farmers, priests and students. ''In the name of God and in the name of this suffering people, whose cries rise to the very heaven and become more tumultuous every day, I beseech you, I beg you, I order you, in the name of God: stop the repression.'' On March 24, 1980, as he celebrated Mass, ''the Monseñor of the people'' was assassinated with a 22-caliber pistol. Ecumenists are those who oppose hostility and brokenness and who call the people of God to their salvation and wholeness.

The day after I wrote the preceding paragraphs, I experienced a powerful event: a day of solidarity with the suffering people of El Salvador, sponsored by the community in which I am living and writing this book, the Ecumenical Institute Bossey just outside Geneva. Through lectures about the repressive situation, through fasting in order to send an offering and through prayers, Bossey students from thirty countries sought to identify with those who are being fiercely wounded by poverty, political savagery, illiteracy and hopelessness. A film by the World Council of Churches told graphically of the torture, secret kidnappings and nonsensical executions that take place daily in this Central American country. All this is done to protect the luxury and privilege of the 2 percent of the population who control practically all of the wealth and resources.

The double tragedy is that most Americans and Canadians do not understand the extent of U.S. military and political involvement in this violence. The United States upholds many regimes and governments which, like that in El Salvador, control by fear and destruction, denying the people's yearning for freedom and justice. Canadian governments take a "what-can-a-small-country-do" attitude and avoid taking stands that might damage Canada-United States relations.

After my encounter with reality in the faces of real people in El Salvador, I am even more sure of two convictions. First, ecumenism —seeking the unity and wholeness of the people of God—involves solidarity with (that is, standing with) those who experience the inhumanity of repression. Injustice is a sign of the deep divisions within humanity and the church. Second, I am convinced that the unity Christ brings, and the only acceptable goal for the church, is one that announces the coming of justice. There is no unity when powerful people continue to preside at the expense of the powerless, or when voiceless people are left out. The true paradigm for the church is unity with justice. By the same token, I believe those who think justice can be achieved without the unity and reconciliation of the church are naïve and are without adequate theological grounds for their witness.

Church Unity and the Poor

Humanity is divided by poverty. Lack of food, shelter and clothing produces anguish and misery and constitutes a major source of human division. Even quarreling among Christians over who are the truly poor (those impoverished in spirit or in body) is itself a vivid reminder that we are divided between those who have much and those who have little.

Again through Archbishop Romero's eyes we can see this spiritual truth. In an address on November 17, 1979 he boldly called the lack of identification with the poor "the sickness of disunity." He was moved to read a confession that had been prepared for the 1978 conference of Latin American bishops gathered at Puebla, Mexico:

> Not all of us in Latin America are sufficiently committed to the poor. We are not always concerned about them or in solidarity with them. Their service demands, in effect, a constant conversion and purification of each Christian toward the attainment of identification, each day more completely, with the poor Christ and with all who are poor.

The beloved archbishop then made his own penetrating comment:

> To me the medicine of our disunity is clear — sincerely to convert ourselves over to the poor. . . . When we are interested in our comforts, our privileges and our advantages, we are not with the poor Christ. There is the source of our division. . . . Let us instead walk again in the path of unity, and the rest will be added to us. Devote yourselves sincerely to the poor. In so doing, you will also be working toward the unity of the Church.[6]

This stance catches many of us off guard, especially if we have never grasped the dehumanizing, fragmenting power of poverty.

Brother Roger Schutz, prior of the Taizé community, also asserts that identifying with the world's poor is central to the ecumenical calling. It is, he says, a *sine qua non* for church renewal, and for getting in touch with the spiritual power of the gospel. Renewal and unity through identifying with the poor have two dimensions, according to Frère Roger: (1) rediscovering, through contact with the poor, the spirit of poverty, that is, a life in which security comes not from the accumulation of material possessions but from our daily dependence upon God; and (2) discovering "a social doctrine of ecumenism," by which he means Christians of all traditions sharing with the poor, working together, participating together in the advancement of human life.[7] Can we see what identifying *with* the poor (not just sending money *to* "those poor people") would do in overcoming divisions, so often socially and economically based, among Christians? It would require that we transform our attitudes toward those we once feared or looked down upon. It would require a humility that comes from depending upon God. It would lead us to share significantly our resources and possessions. "Community cannot exist without visibly sharing possessions," believes Frère Roger.

What happens in the absence of significant and meaningful sharing of resources is well illustrated by the situation of Canada's native people. Increasing industrial development on their lands in the north, coupled with little or no participation by the native people themselves in the planning process is beginning to yield major social, economic, cultural and environmental consequences. The shift in emphasis from renewable to nonrenewable resources is changing the nature of the economy and jeopardizing the native people's ability to control their own economic development. Under the circumstances, the underdevelopment of these people shows signs of being perpetuated indefinitely. What is the appropriate Christian response in such a situation? Several Canadian churches are actively supporting these people in their claims to the land and in pressing their environmental concerns. This is the kind of issue Christians must continue to face as they seek unity with all of humanity.

The church is divided not simply by different doctrines of baptism or different forms of ministry. The church is divided because some of us live in palatial homes while others live in shacks; it is divided because some eat most of the world's protein foods while others eat mostly rice. Some triumphally thank God for all their material blessings while others learn the joy and humility of total reliance on God even for today's essential needs. And some, lacking the most basic necessities of life, are too broken in body and spirit to experience any kind of joy. A church that does not address itself to these gaps cannot experience the unity promised by the one Lord.

Church Unity in a Racially Divided World

What does it mean when people are thought to be inferior or of marginal importance because of their race or ethnic group? What is the meaning of life when both global and local society are structured so that some kinds of people are excluded from certain jobs and responsibilities—for example, when physical qualifications for the job of police officer in the city of Toronto eliminate 95 percent of those Canadians who are of Asian descent? What does it mean when the church participates, even if unconsciously, in racial discrimination—for example, by holding stock in corporations that continue to do business with South Africa, or by maintaining accounts in banks that have investments there?

CHRISTIAN UNITY: MATRIX FOR MISSION

These questions point to racism — discrimination against and stereotyping of persons on the basis of their racial origins — as a terribly divisive element in the world and in the Christian church. In condemning it the ecumenical movement has clearly confessed racism as a theological heresy, a perversion of God's will in creation. To quote a world consultation on racism:

> Every human being, created in the image of God, is a person for whom Christ died. Racism, which is the use of a person's racial origins to determine the person's value, is an assault on *Christ's* values and a rejection of *His* sacrifice. Wherever it appears, whether in the individual or in the collective, it is sin. It must be openly fought by all those who are on Christ's side, and by the Church as the designated vehicle and instrument of Christ's purpose in the world.[8]

This ecumenical statement calls our attention to two crucial aspects of racism. First, it is a sin against Christ. The struggle against racism is a Christian imperative; it is a response to the One who obliterated all human divisions by giving his life upon a cross. Second, racism is also a violation of the church's order. Although, as the Bible reveals, the church is called to be a sign of God's love to an unreconciled humanity, this purpose is still unfulfilled. In fact, "our experience shows that denominationalism and racism have destroyed the unity of the Church . . . the sin of racism contradicts the nature of the Church and its oneness which we confess."[9] The Christian community is visibly broken; its life as a community is organized according to prejudice and exclusion by race. In short, whatever divides the world also tragically divides the church.

In the United States, one ecumenical arena in which racism and visible unity have been confronted in depth, and with hope and trust, is the Consultation on Church Union (COCU). Among the ten churches seeking a "truly catholic, truly evangelical, and truly reformed" united church are three predominantly black churches — African Methodist Episcopal, African Methodist Episcopal Zion and Christian Methodist Episcopal — whose histories go back to slavery and the subsequent battle for freedom in the United States. When the racial crisis of the late 1960s struck American Christianity, the providential participation of these three bodies allowed COCU to become a test case of the prospects for reconciliation beyond racism. Both the intensity of COCU's debates and the sweetness of its fruits lie in the fact that here churches are actually seeking to become truly united, to exhibit a common life that is just and to overcome divisions of race and class in the church's order. COCU deliberately aims to be "in the vanguard of the struggle for the 'New Community'."[10]

This commitment was writ large when in 1970 COCU issued for study *A Plan of Union for the Church of Christ Uniting*. This document presented the consensus reached after eight years on those classic church-dividing issues related to faith, sacraments, membership and ministry. In addition, a proposed structure for the uniting church tried to address directly the racial divisions of the church in the United States and to struggle toward an inclusive Christian fellowship. Two sections among many in the *Plan of Union* reveal the commitment to make church union a true reconciliation for the sake of humankind:

> Special care must be taken to show no discrimination among members because of race. Membership in all aspects of the church's life will be open to persons of all racial and ethnic groups.[11]

> The united church believes that racism is the denial of the demands of the Fatherhood of God, that it negates the concepts of one Lord and one humanity, that it inflicts upon the helpless poverty, ignorance, despair, and hopelessness. Congregations, individuals, or groups of Christians who exclude, exploit or patronize any of their fellowmen, however subtly, offend God and place the profession of their faith in doubt.[12]

The *Plan of Union* then made a specific — and very dramatic — proposal that the congregations at the local level form themselves into "parishes," local fellowships that would include congregations of different traditions, especially black and white. As envisioned, the parish's life would focus upon regular joint celebrations of the Lord's Supper, the working of the ministers from the various congregations in team relationships and the common sharing of resources and decision making as expressed through a local parish council.

This *Plan of Union*, and particularly the parish concept, proved to be both one of the most creative and one of the most controversial ecumenical proposals ever made. Following debates, the structural proposals were rejected so thoroughly by the churches that the plan was withdrawn. What is instructive for us is that the negative judgments came from both black and white Christians, but for different reasons.

Among the predominantly white churches the *Plan of Union* attracted any number of criticisms, including fears that it would lead to "a monolithic church" and loss of denominational identity, and reflecting distrust of any structural union. For the most part, the churches affirmed the achieved theological consensus as sound Christian teaching and as offering a fruitful basis for the eventual union of these churches. (This positive reality is often ignored by COCU's opponents.) As one who was deeply involved in those events, I am convinced that a major reason for all the negative responses, however, was a deep uncertainty about the kind of racial inclusiveness envisaged by COCU. The Consultation concretely challenged racism, and uncovered some of the defenses of this evil that exist in the structures of American society and churches.

The minimal responses from the predominantly black churches indicated that blacks could not accept the importance of a theological consensus around issues that did not address the front-and-center divisions of their daily experience. For example, the constitutions and liturgies of the three black Methodist churches are identical in language with those of The United Methodist Church, from which they had divided. But consensus in language or constitutional documents has not produced unity in living fellowship among Methodists. Black Christians have experienced so much discrimination at the hands of white Christians in the towns and cities where they live that they look with suspicion upon any proposal of union with those same people. They rightly asked, "How can we expect to be brothers and sisters of equal status in the Church of Christ Uniting when the members of the majority refuse to live next door as neighbors? How can we have 'brotherhood' and 'sisterhood' without 'neighborhood'?"[13] The logic for black Christians was simple: unless there is more evidence of true reconciliation, including repentance, any ecumenical relationship would result in divisive and demoralizing consequences for the black experience, institutions and community. Hence, they would accept no church unity that would result "in the elimination of leadership and the loss of black self-control, absorption and the loss of identity, accommodation and the loss of self-reliance."[14]

The call is for a unity with diversity, equity and shared power. That is the explicit goal which COCU and other ecumenical bodies continue to pursue, although in many respects these churches have only begun to find the capacity for racial inclusiveness. Before them are several unresolved issues of conscience and theology, such as the place of racial identity, including theology and forms of worship, within the legitimate diversity of Christian identity; the search for a form of church order that can accommodate tensions like those experienced in the past fifteen years between whites and not only black, but yellow and red peoples, too; and a form of church union with multiple structures. Admittedly all the required answers and commitments are not yet at hand, but the emerging image of this sort of church unity is serving the cause of Christian reconciliation in a thrilling though difficult way.

One other clue may help those who wish to go beyond simply "combating racism" — though that is an essential task — to living together in a reconciled community. When *racism* ceases to be an abstract concept and becomes live men and women and children across the table—people who can tell how racism, on both personal and institutional levels, has scarred their lives—then our salvation is nearer. We must experience and confess personal aspects of the divisiveness of racism. Racism ruins human lives. And we must realize that more than doctrinal agreements will be required if that broken fellowship is to be restored.

The hope of ecumenism lies in Christians of all colors who, under their common Lord, can be both gentle and angry with one another when necessary, but who know deep in their hearts that their unity is already secured in the blood of Christ. I truly believe that the extent to which I can transcend my racism today is due primarily, not to sociological analyses or educational processes, as vitally constructive as these are, but to persons like Walter Bingham, Frederick Jordan, E.P. Murchison, Rosa Page Welch, Clyde Williams, Willie Greer and a host of other black Christians who beheld my insensitivities but nonetheless nurtured and befriended me. This is the gracious way God offers healing to a racially divided people.

Church Unity and the Disabled

One of my family's best friends lives in two places — in the Berkshires of Western Massachusetts and on that heavenly crooked finger known as Cape Cod. Among other things, Ginnie is a tenacious local ecumenist, challenging parochialisms of all varieties and admonishing the quick and the dead to listen to Christ's high-priestly prayer (John 17) and to do something about it. Her efforts grow out of a sensitivity to the reconciling power of the Holy Spirit, which heals both the arrogance and loneliness that mark so many lives. Since 1978 Ginnie has been witnessing to unity from a wheelchair, or more accurately, from a wheelchair and the slow two-step she courageously does with her stricken limbs. She is the victim of two paralyzing strokes.

In her present condition, Ginnie helps me understand that persons with disabilities are also the victims of another paralysis. This is the paralysis caused by the fear and prejudice of many people against the

CHRISTIAN UNITY: MATRIX FOR MISSION

strange, the unusual, the "abnormal"; a paralysis stemming from the insensitivities of architects and members of church boards who assume that all who enter the house of God will be walking, stepping, talking, seeing, hearing and fully capable of caring for themselves. It is the paralysis caused by the condescending silence of those who "cannot bear another caucus group demanding their human rights." Being friends with the new Ginnie, reborn in pain, has taught me how alienated and isolated disabled people feel. Attitudes toward them are fragmenting the church and alienating good human beings from society. I am convinced that new lessons on ecumenism await those who have a friend like Ginnie. Our definitions and symbols of wholeness and health and success will get broken, but will be put together again in a stronger manner.

Listen to a group of Christians who believe the disabled are a clue to the unity of the church and of humanity:

> The Church cannot exemplify "the full humanity revealed in Christ," bear witness to the interdependence of humankind or achieve unity in diversity if it continues to acquiesce in the social isolation of disabled persons and to deny them full participation in life. The unity of the family of God is handicapped where these brothers and sisters are treated as objects of condescending charity. It is broken where they are left out.[15]

I heard this point intellectually in 1971 at a Faith and Order conference at Louvain, Belgium. Yet only now do I begin to know what it means. In rereading the Louvain declaration, we see that it carries the essence of the gospel, both for the disabled and for the churches:

> The presence of the handicapped as part of the human community is both a call to the strong to help the weak to overcome their limitations, and also a reminder to the strong of the limitations which beset all human life, threatened as it is by evil and bounded by death. Both the weak and the strong have to learn to accept as well as to overcome their limitations. The victory of Christ over death assures us that there is no limit to the power of God to overcome all that threatens us.[16]

The handicapped have learned to recognize their weaknesses and their strengths and to make the best of their limited powers and resources. As such they can teach others, particularly the church, how God's resources can enter human life and bless the world through the recognition of weakness. They can teach us an immeasurable lesson about the wholeness of life, namely how to continue the struggle against evil while still trusting and hoping.

Louvain asked some probing questions that are still the agenda of the churches and of the ecumenical movement: Do we penalize the handicapped in our practices of baptism, confirmation or Holy Communion? Do we marginalize them and their leadership in ordinations and the election of officers in the church? Do we make it practically possible for the handicapped to participate as regularly and fully as they are able in the life of our congregations and meetings? Does their inclusion influence the church's worship in prayers and in forgiveness, as well as in its architecture and physical facilities?

Let us ask one more question. Our awareness of the needs of the handicapped has been increased during the International Year of Disabled Persons, with at least some positive results. After seeing, especially in Canada, government, business, the arts and the media all taking the International Year of Disabled Persons seriously, we might ask what the church has learned. What concrete ramps (instead of steps) are we going to take to be sure that what has been learned this year is not lost?

The handicapped are indeed important to our doctrine of the church. They bring us profound insights about the church as a sign of unity and wholeness to humankind. Through them we learn that the church is always a marginal community, limited and often powerless by worldly standards. But we learn also that marginalization is ultimately seen and expressed in the cross as our victory.

Church Unity and the Alienation Between Women and Men

The final church-dividing concern we shall consider is sexism, the alienation between women and men arising from discrimination and exploitation based on sex. Many a battle has been fought—and some won — in recent years over ''male-dominated churches and societies.'' While this situation yields to no facile solutions, nor are there easy agreements about the implications, the fact is that the churches in the United States, Canada and other countries are faced with a ''polarizing sexism that permeates the language and practice of worship, theology, styles of ministry, and the governing structures of all denominations.''[17] In such a situation COCU was honest enough to confess the gravity of this alienating liability to the future unity of the church.

The Consultation may live its way toward union, therefore—only to discover within five to ten years that many of its members have been so alienated along the way that ''unity'' has become a gentlemen's agreement within the dominant group, rather than agreement of partners who have struggled together toward true mutuality in every expression of their personal and institutional lives.[18]

It is no secret that dealing with sexism is like walking through an ecumenical minefield. The intensity of the polarization between men and women, involving pros and cons on both sides, is as heated as any other church-dividing issue we face. Fortunately, the pivotal issues have already been identified by the partners in dialogue and furnish the churches with the agenda for both theological study and diplomacy aimed at achieving genuine mutuality. Roles and styles of leadership (less hierarchical and more collegial), the abuse of the Bible in biblical interpretation (assuming women should keep quiet in the church and stay ''in their place''), the language and symbols used in theology and worship (which in the past reflected the imagery of men) are all parts of this agenda.

The most controversial theological issue relates to the ordination of ministers and revolves around the question of whether women can be validly ordained to the ministry of word and sacraments. For some churches the ordination of women is contrary to official dogmatic teaching and thus threatens, in their judgment, the unity of the church. For others any consensus on the practice of ministry that does not allow for the full participation of women and men together is considered ''an act of disunity against humankind.''[19] The Roman Catholic Church and the Orthodox churches—Eastern and Oriental— flatly deny ordination to women. Anglicans (the worldwide name for Episcopalians) are divided: in the United States, Canada, New Zealand and Hong Kong ordination is conferred upon men and women alike; other parts of the Anglican communion, including the Church of England, presently deny ordination to women or have postponed the decision until a later date. The record of Protestant churches, while in most cases officially for inclusive ordination, is not without blemish.

Mainline Protestant churches in North America and Europe have some experience with ordained women, but their theology is made suspect by their placement practices. Women are ordained but only, it seems, for service in small rural congregations or as associates in multiple staffs. No, the issue is before *all* the churches, although with different degrees of intensity. Likewise the dialogue — which, granted, is in its early stages — must be pursued with respect for different cultural milieus.

The exploration of sexism, however, begins and ends with a theological conviction that implies concrete changes: ''The Church's unity includes women and men in a true mutuality. . . . The relations of women and men must be shaped by reciprocity and not by subordination. The unity of the Church requires that women be free to live out the gift which God has given to them and to respond to their calling to share fully in the life and witness of the Church.''[20]

THE BOTTOM LINE: A NEW URGENCY FOR CHURCH UNITY

These acknowledged church-dividing issues bring to the fore both a time-honored adage and a fresh discovery. They remind us that the church's unity is a sign of the unity of the world; those who hold the Christian vision of unity agonize over the fact that broken relationships within the body of Christ are reflected in a divided, warring humanity. This insight is a tremendous gain. But two warnings are critical as we live out the ecumenical vision.

First, none of the fragmenting realities we discussed earlier and its reconciliation is the whole gospel unto itself, not even all five taken together. To treat one human problem as if it enveloped all God's truth for our time would be to create another heresy — that is, identifying the full gospel of Jesus Christ with any partial expression of it. Each one—racism, sexism or whichever—offers a glimpse of what fullness in Christ is and can be, but it cannot claim to say all there is to say about God's love and grace.

Second, it is a tempting heresy to assume that one of the two—the unity of the church or the unity of humankind—can be left out of a loyal ecumenical commitment. Some people, including even some dedicated church leaders, assume that the urgency of dealing with the catalog of human hostilities and divisions that today require our response makes the search for Christian unity obsolete. Unity can therefore, they think, easily be dropped from the agenda and budget. This has been shown repeatedly to be a naive and counterproductive assumption, whether it is made in ecumenical bodies, church program units, theological seminaries, or wherever decisions of Christian conscience and policy are being formed. On the contrary, to face the disunity of humankind with integrity will require an even more deliberate and consecrated commitment to Christian unity. Why? Because the same issues and the same people that keep visible unity from happening in the churches will also thwart a genuine confronting of the disunity of the global community.

CHRISTIAN UNITY: MATRIX FOR MISSION

Those who resist the overcoming of church divisions will, with equal power and strategy, oppose any proposals for change in the world's economic order or political alliances; they will avoid any reconciling solidarity with the world of suffering and agony. The same nuances of selfishness and the same powers and principalities preside over both options. Those who will not entrust their Christian identity and power to the reconciling acts of church unity will not risk the loss of status and privilege in order to identify with the poor and the oppressed. Those ecumenical strategists who assume otherwise will be terribly surprised when the moment of truth arrives. In a real sense the unity of the church and the unity of the human family are inseparably bound together. Only through unity and communion within its own life can Christianity witness to the peace and love of God in this disturbed, oppressed and divided world.

This conclusion does not put the church on a triumphalist pedestal. It only recalls the church, through its own unity, to be a sign and sacrament to all humankind of the ultimate unity of God's reconciling and redeeming purpose. When the church denies that divinely given unity, it becomes not a sign but a countersign to the world. Church unity, therefore, is a calling we cannot lay aside, except as an act of unfaithfulness to the gospel. Bringing about the unity of the church and the unity of humankind is the most urgent ministry facing Christians in their local and global responsibilities.

6 Spirituality and Ecumenism

On December 11, 1965 a united church was about to be born in Nigeria, a nation on the brink of civil war. Ninety-five years of dialogue and carefully laid plans were about to bring forth a new day for Christianity in that African country. But the child was stillborn; church union never took place. The ecumenical movement was startled by last-minute acts of Christian alienation in a country so urgently in need of a sign of conciliation. Tribal and ethnic jealousies, fears about property, rivalry over who would be bishops and rumors that distorted facts carried the day. Among the explanations that came from Nigeria, the judgment of the Anglican archbishop pointed to the fundamental cause: "Our churches are not yet spiritually mature enough to be united."[1]

This judgment could be made about the church in many places. In the United States and Canada, Mexico, Scotland, New Zealand, France, the Middle East and other places, Christians have rebelled against unity by keeping others at a safe distance. But rather than merely bemoan this fact, we need to be aware of the deeper reality: at the heart of Christian unity is a genuine Christian spirituality, which nurtures and empowers.

This, I am convinced, is the most important insight for the ecumenical movement today — and the most neglected. Lethargy, fatigue, frustration and off-center strategies are not the primary factors stalling the dynamic movement toward the fulfillment of Christ's prayer for unity. They are merely symptoms of a spiritual poverty that plagues the churches. Frère Roger Schutz of Taizé unveils this condition when he observes that many pastors, bishops and Christians of all sorts allow their heavy responsibilities or their spiritual laziness to keep them from finding time for communion with God: "Churchmen [and women] like these, overloaded with work, think that the first essential is to carry out their most immediate duties. Lack of time sometimes makes them give up dialogue with

77

God. The overdevelopment of activities no longer allows them time for the vital withdrawal into God."[2]

Any advocate of unity recognizes the truth in Schutz's statement. We have only to watch and listen to those who half-heartedly attend ecumenical meetings. Christians cannot hope to be peacemakers unless they are, above all else, men and women with a deep drive toward spiritual living, seeking to know Christ in their days and their nights. Unless fed by the springs of a continuing encounter with Christ, we become impatient or disillusioned, pedantic advocates or bureaucrats preoccupied with power. In the final sermon he preached before his death in 1958, Bishop George K.A. Bell appealed for "more saintly lives." Speaking about the World Council of Churches as one who helped give it life, he said:

> The work of the World Council promoting the visible unity of the church will be most likely to prosper, if the facts of revelation on which it is founded are supported by the spiritual witness of dedicated Christian lives; and if, both at the heart of the central organizations, and in all our various congregations and churches, the call to devotion and holiness is obeyed, as the saints have obeyed it in all periods of Christian history.[3]

My point is this: the power toward unity comes from living in the presence of God.

The word *spirituality* evokes an image of a monk or nun living a cloistered life. That witness should not be discarded too quickly as "not for us" or discounted among the many forms of ministry used by God. In this chapter, however, *spirituality* means not merely the activities of monks, nuns and mystics, but the calling of everyone, a calling that includes a variety of approaches and spiritual procedures. It means a personal and corporate communion with God through Christ, given by the Holy Spirit and leading to a life motivated by God's will. Such a spirituality is marked by prayer, devotional readings, adoration, repentance, forgiveness, sharing the Eucharist or the Lord's Supper, meditation and theological reflection. Out of this seedbed genuine ecumenism flowers and takes shape in the world.

The real problem of the ecumenical movement is a deep sense of alienation among Christians. What really divides Christians, as well as other people, is that we are estranged from ourselves, from society and from God. We live in the midst of distrust and division instead of the love and affection ordained by God. "It is our sins, the personal or communal obstacles that we put in the way, which prevent the miracle of unity bursting forth.''[4] We can only change this situation by renewing the springs of authentic spirituality and letting our communion with God transform our relations with others. This kind of renewal is not easy; it comes through spiritual struggle. But only so shall we be able to bridge the chasms that divide the churches. We shall learn that God invites us to live the whole life in the whole community given in Christ. ''We are unfinished humans until we consent to that power of the Spirit and are drawn into a wholeness of being.''[5]

I write these words in Rome, only a kilometer or so from the Basilica of St. Peter where Vatican Council II (1962-1965) issued the landmark *Decree on Ecumenism*. That history-making council called for a deeper ''spiritual ecumenism,'' and cited implications of what this means. ''There can be no ecumenism worthy of the name without a change of heart. For it is from newness of attitudes (cf. Eph. 4:23), from self-denial and unstinted love, that yearnings for unity take their rise and grow toward maturity'' (Paragraph 7). Then came the conclusion: ''This change of heart and holiness of life, along with public and private prayer for the unity of Christians, should be regarded as the soul of the whole ecumenical movement'' (Paragraph 8). ''Newness of attitudes,'' ''a change of heart,'' an authentic life of holiness —these are not just personal attributes. They are the fruits of Christian spirituality, which make possible a renewed and reconciled church.

PRAYING FOR UNITY

The ecumenical life is above all a life of prayer, both personal and corporate. The World Council of Churches accepted this discipline early in its life: ''The measure of our concern for unity is the degree to which we pray for it. We cannot expect God to give us unity unless we prepare ourselves to receive his gift by costly and purifying prayer. To pray *together* is to be drawn together.''[6] The first ecumenical action of divided Christians, says Maurice Villain, the revered Roman Catholic ecumenist, should be not to organize a discussion or pass a resolution but ''to kneel down together at the foot of the cross of our common Savior, in a mood of repentance, for we are all sinners before him, we all are guilty in some way or another of the faults of separation.''[7] Admittedly, this is not the typical image of what it means to be ecumenical. We would rather assume that the first act is to appoint a high-powered ecumenical committee, to begin some social program, or to be asked to make a jet trip to some far-away place—all, of course, in the interest of Christian unity. But if we are to say something worth saying when the appointment does come or the right meeting is convened, we must be prepared. Only as Christians purify their hearts can they find the grace to overcome prejudices, hatreds or lethargy. Douglas V. Steere's truth applies particularly to ecumenism: "Nothing could more directly redeem the times, restore the sense of the divine image that lives in each human being, and lift the inward and outward sense of responsibility of men and women for each other than a rekindling of these deepest ranges of prayer."[8] Prayer for unity in this case takes place not only at great and exceptional moments, but in the ordinary events of daily life. Therefore, prayer is, in the mind of historian Ruth Rouse, "the main spring of ecumenical advance, without which ecumenical activities would be useless if not dangerous."[9]

The globe-trotting ecumenical giant John R. Mott used to spend every seventh day in prayer and spiritual renewal, regardless of where he was. Persons like Mott understand the Jewish practice of *chipat,* whereby every seventh year the land was allowed to rest before being seeded again, to be renewed for future usefulness. The day of prayer was not an idle gesture by this great Methodist layman who out-ran, out-talked and out-led his generation. Mott knew the importance of prayer for neophytes and veterans alike and made it his rule of life.

Eastern Orthodox Christians have a centuries-old practice that could be widely beneficial. As a response to Paul's injunction to pray without ceasing, many Orthodox several times a day offer the so-called Jesus Prayer, which pleads: "Lord Jesus Christ, Son of God, have pity on me, a sinner." The constant repetition of this prayer across the centuries has kept believers close to Christ and aware of the daily need for mercy and reconciliation. From Advent to Pentecost the Taizé Community includes another simple petition in their evening prayers: "Lord, grant that all Christians may again find visible unity, that they may all be one so that the world may believe." Think how much closer we would be to transforming the world's division into unity if millions — pastors and laypeople, secretaries and denominational presidents, mothers and daughters — would pray that simple prayer once every day.

Prayer does not merely prepare us for the real ecumenical task; prayer *is* the ecumenical task. "Prayer is not only a way of asking for unity; it is itself a way of achieving it . . . prayer not only pleads for unity, it unites."[10] Once we learn to walk in God's presence, we will feel the pain and agony of disunity. We will realize, as Patriarch

Filaret, the nineteenth-century Russian Orthodox Patriarch of Moscow, said, that "the walls of division do not reach to heaven." We will taste the joy of unity given to those who follow Christ.

Clearly the church's prayers for unity can reach new depths if we turn often to Christ's majestic prayer as recorded in John 17. Here the Lord stands before the throne of God interceding for us. To be able to pray Christ's words, asking God the Holy Spirit to put in our hearts and on our lips the intention of Jesus Christ when he prayed "that they may all be one; even as thou, Father, art in me, and I in thee, that they also may be in us, so that the world may believe that thou hast sent me" (John 17:21) is the pinnacle of prayer. From inside an authentic spirituality this prayer becomes not a text for exegesis or an instant plug for whatever ecumenical project we are pushing, but our personal entrance into Christ's life of serving and reconciling love. To pray thus requires that we entrust ourselves (egos, defenses, ambitions — all) and our traditions (blessed diversities, theological disagreements—all) completely to Christ, that we become open to his will. We become ready to see Christ in others, to love one another as he loves each and to be changed by love through repentance. When more and more people begin to pray in this manner, the unity of the church for the sake of humanity will be brought nearer.

CONTEMPLATIVE ECUMENISM

Another dimension of spirituality for Christian unity is contemplation. Again, a caveat is necessary. Contemplation is often assumed to be a ritual for those in monasteries and convents, and thereby inapplicable and unavailable to ordinary folk. But contemplation — intense prayer, meditation, spiritual reflection, solitude — is available to every Christian and is your and my calling. Indeed, it is part of our salvation from the frantic pace of modern life, which drains our spirits in countless ways and lures us to become self-sufficient (that is, not needing God), isolated persons.

I deeply believe the ecumenical vocation can be empowered by contemplation. This conviction has come to me from two sources: first, my encounter, through reading and conversations, with such contemporary contemplatives as Thomas Merton (American Roman Catholic), Roger Schutz (French Protestant) and Henri Nouwen (Dutch Roman Catholic). They have shown me the unlimited spiritual reservoir that God offers through a life punctuated by prayer, meditation and silence. Second, nearly twenty-five years in active ecumenical work have revealed to me that only a spiritually-based presence can give us the patience and power to keep our wits in the midst of painful delays, interminable committee meetings and the myriad haunting fears and hesitations. Once we get in touch with our own interior life and catch a glimpse of other people's commitments and resources, it is obvious that church unity is betrayed not only by theological and nontheological factors but by a lack of spiritual direction. So often delegates come to meetings without souls. We try to design unity — or avoid unity — by our own proclamations. Contemplation teaches us that unity comes essentially from listening to God in silence; it is fed by expectation as we await the word of God. Contemplation must therefore become a touchstone in our praxis toward Christian unity.

Thomas Merton, the glad monk from the Abbey of Gethsemani, near Bardstown, Kentucky, once said: "The deepest level of communication is not communication, but communion."[11] This speaks volumes about ecumenical methodologies. Our dialogues and negotiations, our work in councils of churches rarely get beyond "taking the mote out of our neighbor's eye" because our conversations and cooperative efforts are being pursued in the context of insecurity rather than communion. For Merton life, including the journey toward Christian unity, is a continuous search for communion with God in order to manifest God to and be reconciled with other men and women. In what we might now read as his epitaph, Merton once said about himself: "Whatever I may have written, I think it all can be reduced in the end to this one root truth: that God calls human persons to union with Himself and with one another in Christ, in the Church which is his Mystical Body."[12]

Contemplation—silent meditation—is not just a matter of sitting still, as if this has magic power to solve our ecumenical problems. The Holy Spirit does not come simply to those who are quiet for a while. Prayer and meditation involve reaching for a new orientation. "Instead of being directed toward ends we have chosen ourselves, instead of being measured by the profit and pleasure we judge they will produce, our own efforts are more and more directed to an obedient and cooperative submission to grace, which implies first of all an increasingly attentive and receptive attitude toward the hidden action of the Holy Spirit."[13]

Nor is contemplation simply introspection. Introspection, which plagues many people in our society, means looking exclusively inward, getting in touch with our feelings, carefully analyzing our thoughts and emotions. While this can be constructive, it can also be dangerous. Introspection, as Henri Nouwen shows, can "entangle us in the labyrinth of our own ideas, feelings, and emotions,'' thus paralyzing us with unproductive worries about ourselves and turning our lives into orgies of self-gratification.[14] The popular word for all this is "narcissism," complete preoccupation with ourselves. Contemplation, on the other hand, means turning away from ourselves, offering all that we are to God in the simple trust that through God's loving care all will be made new.

In a sentence, contemplation is the transforming of ourselves from selfishness to fellowship with God in Christ. We no longer see ourselves as radical individuals with no need of others. Instead, we acknowledge that we are dependent on Another; we belong to a universal community that graciously enfolds us with those we once viewed as occasional acquaintances, opponents and even enemies. Here the potential for vital Christian unity breaks forth. As we begin to dispel selfishness, the root of so much division, we become able to live in unity with other people. This transformation into communion with God makes possible acceptance of those who differ with, and are different from, ourselves. Goals, ambitions, definitions of success are no longer self-centered; they are centered in God. This was the divine "Aha" that made Paul able to say in faith: "I have been crucified with Christ; it is no longer I who live, but Christ who lives in me" (Gal. 2:20). It is the death of the selfish you, the power-seeking you, the you who finds intimacy difficult to share with others because you seek control rather than union. It is the birth of the new and liberated self with a new capacity to love; the birth of a people who see the church in more comprehensive terms, and who are able to act together with other Christians in the Spirit.

Ecumenism then is based on union with a loving God who frees and animates us to seek union in faith and fellowship, in witness and service with other children of God. This magnificent realization is both mystical and practical.

By now it should be clear that contemplation and prayer do not mean being absent from the world or running away from the realities of life. "They are for and within a world of action," says Merton. They are "a way of looking at our neighbor; a way of looking which is transfigured by reconciliation."[15] Hostile nations, divided churches, broken families, lonely people living side by side but in isolation—these remain. But contemplation and prayer give us the chance to see and judge them from God's perspective. We are equipped with what Anglican theologian David Jenkins once called "spirituality for combat." Without such a spirituality the battle for a new creation in persons and the church is lost; with this spirituality the church can witness against provincialism, hatred and distrust and can experience the fullness of God's grace.

THE WEEK OF PRAYER FOR CHRISTIAN UNITY

Prayer for the unity of all Christians is dramatically observed during the week of January 18 to 25 each year. Protestants, Roman Catholics and Eastern Orthodox come together in cathedrals and village churches to pray for their coming unity. This annual celebration is a clear example of ecumenical spirituality, and its potential, after seventy-five years, is still not fully realized.

The movement for worldwide prayer grew in several places. Various nineteenth-century groups took the cause as their primary purpose, but not until the early twentieth century did it really begin to find acceptance in the churches. At the turn of the century two Anglican priests called for an Octave (eight days) of prayer for unity. Spencer Jones from England was one of these priests; his book *England and the Holy See; An Essay Toward Reunion* created no little controversy, but also issued the call for prayer, suggesting that Christians pray on St. Peter's day (June 29) each year for unity between the Church of England and the Roman Catholic Church. A more substantial initiative came from an American Episcopal priest, Lewis Thomas Wattson, who proposed that a full eight days be devoted to prayers for Christian unity annually, according to the Roman Catholic liturgical calendar, from the Feast of St. Peter's Chair (January 18), to the Feast of the Conversion of St. Paul (January 25). Wattson, like Jones, focused upon corporate reunion between Anglicans and Roman Catholics, accompanied by the acceptance of the primacy of the Pope. Assuming the religious name of Father Paul of Graymoor (the monastery near Peekskill, New York), Wattson and an Episcopal nun, Lurana White, founded a religious order named the Society of the Atonement. Its purpose was to work and pray for Christian unity, or as Wattson put it, at-one-ment.

In 1908 Wattson and his small order were received into the Roman Catholic Church. Since Jones and Wattson emphasized unity by return to Rome, their Church Unity Octave was endorsed by three popes but was viewed with understandable skepticism by Protestants. By the time Father Paul died in 1940, the Society of the Atonement had become an articulate ecumenical voice within the Roman Catholic Church, notably through its publications, and the Week of Prayer for Christian Unity had become a profound witness to the search for unity among the churches.

A French priest, Abbé (Father) Paul Couturier, modified and enlarged the spirit of the Octave in order to make it truly ecumenical. This priest from Lyons had a truly irenic heart and understood the offense to Protestants of the earlier model. He wrote, "Neither Catholic prayer, nor Orthodox prayer, nor Anglican prayer, nor Protestant prayer suffice. All of them are necessary, and all of them together."[16] As an act of courtesy, Couturier changed the title from *octave* (a Roman Catholic term) to the Universal *Week* of Prayer for Christian Unity.

He also believed it must be more than an annual 1. Under his inspiration the content of the prayers was altered to lift up the sins of disunity as acts in which all churches have participated. Roman Catholics, Protestants and Orthodox should pray together for forgiveness for their divisions and for the restoration of visible unity. Abbé Couturier's classic prayer exemplified an inclusive spirit: "May our Lord grant to His Church on earth that peace and unity which were in His mind and purpose when, on the eve of His passion, He prayed 'that all might be one'." In a more popular formula, congregations began to pray "for the unity of the Church of Jesus Christ, as He wills and when He wills." Couturier believed that prayer is necessary to resolve theological problems and sought to increase the spirit of prayer in each church as a means of spiritual renewal. In his view each church would need to be renewed before reconciliation could take place. This inclusive version of the week, first launched at Lyons in 1933, became very successful and spread around the world with the gracious imprimatur of Abbé Couturier.

To complete the picture of the development of the week of prayer, we must record the early efforts of the Faith and Order movement of the World Council of Churches, largely at the initiative of its ingenious secretary, the Episcopal layman Robert H. Gardiner. In 1913 the Faith and Order Commission — still in process of formation — issued a leaflet on *Prayer and Unity* (anonymously written by Gardiner), calling upon the churches to pray for their unity on Pentecost Sunday. In 1915 a manual on prayer for unity was published. Then in 1920, at the acclaimed Preparatory Conference on Faith and Order in Geneva, the infant movement decided to promote a special week of prayer for church unity, ending on Pentecost Sunday, as one of its early priorities. In 1949 Faith and Order moved its dates from Pentecost to January 18 to 25, thus insuring that Roman Catholics, Orthodox and Protestants could all pray together during the same week.

CHRISTIAN UNITY: MATRIX FOR MISSION

Since the days of Abbé Couturier's and Faith and Order's separate initiatives, the Week of Prayer has been celebrated in towns and cities throughout the world, and has included joint worship services, public meetings and various acts of cooperation. In simple and dramatic ways these occasions contribute to the sharing of different liturgies and to the building of new friendship among the churches. The Week of Prayer always serves as a barometer of the passion for unity, which reads sometimes high and sometimes only low. But in countless places it has widened and deepened relations among the churches, and given hope for the future. What is often forgotten is that such an ecumenical event has to be reinterpreted and reemphasized in each generation. The most imminent danger, however, is the temptation to eliminate the sense of divine anguish at the divisions among Christians and thus to pray for unity without an urgent sense that God and God's people should expect visible unity actually to happen. The Week of Prayer for Christian Unity, says Maurice Villain, "demands men and women of energy so moved by the tragedy of Christian Unity that they can no longer rest in peace. But they must be endowed with what Fr. Couturier liked to call 'prudent boldness'."[17] Our prayers for unity in Christ must be incarnate in the lives of the churches.

CENTERS OF ECUMENICAL FORMATION

Let us now discuss some of the centers where a spirituality of ecumenism is at work in the world, and especially where ecumenical workers and leaders are being equipped. Ecumenical encounters — through retreat centers, academic courses and workshops—are pivotal for the work ahead. The task of forming ecumenical leaders becomes even more crucial now that many theological seminaries have abdicated their functions as centers of education for ecumenism, especially in sharing history, information and technical training for participation in the ecumenical movement.

We shall mention three European centers — Taizé, Grandchamp and Bossey—and a fourth particularly North American expression of the ecumenical spirit, the Ecumenical Summer Mission Conferences. Each of these illustrates in its own way the kind of encounter that is an essential part of the ecumenical task.

The Community of Taizé
One of the most dynamic and heralded places for Christian unity and renewal is Taizé, an ecumenical monastic community in a small

French village in Burgundy. This rural campus, dotted with retreat houses, tents, converted milking sheds and a huge concrete chapel of modern design, attracts thousands upon thousands of pilgrims for unity each year. They come to share in Taizé's gift—*l'allégresse de l'aujourd'hui,* the joy of today.

Taizé is the inspiration of Roger Schutz who, as a theological student of the Swiss Reformed Church, over forty years ago had a dream of a reformed monasticism that could relate to the modern world and bridge the divisions among the churches. In 1940, after his seminary days at Lausanne, this frail but spiritually motivated pastor traveled to Burgundy to visit relatives and to seek a location for his sanctuary for Christian unity. He went first to Cluny, the ruins of the once great Benedictine center where Peter the Venerable and others brought new life into the Roman Catholic Church. While at Cluny, Schutz learned that a dilapidated farmhouse was for sale a few miles away in the poverty-stricken village of Taizé. Wanting to look around the village and think about the house, Schutz asked a poor old woman where he might find an inn. She told him there was none, but invited him to "Come and eat with me." Several days later, after hearing of the young pastor's plans, the old woman entreated, "Stay with us, we are so lonely."

Roger Schutz accepted his Macedonian call and bought the house. For two years he lived alone, visiting the people in the village and praying the daily offices three times a day. Then, as Hitler and the Nazis swept across Europe, Schutz began to use his house as a way station for Jews and other refugees in flight to nearby Switzerland. During one of Schutz's clandestine trips to Geneva, the Nazis occupied all of France and the French-Swiss border was closed. He moved into an apartment in Geneva with Max Thurian—later to become one of the architects of Taizé and the community's theologian—and two other students. Together they began to give shape and color to the emerging ecumenically-oriented monastic community. Their worship was held in a chapel of the commanding Reformed Cathedral of St. Pierre in Geneva. In 1944 when France was liberated the group returned to Taizé; and on Easter, 1949 the first seven brothers (*frères*) took their sacred vows, with Frère Roger becoming the prior. Since that day Taizé has been a vital presence for unity in the world.

The goal of Taizé is church unity as a sign for the reconciling of all humanity. Frère Roger included this fundamental principle in the community's rule: "Be consumed with burning zeal for the unity of the Body of Christ."[18] In interpreting Taizé's origins he later wrote: "In establishing at Taizé a common life at the heart of Protestantism, we have no other intention than to bring together men who wish to commit themselves to follow in the footsteps of Christ in order to be a living sign of the Church's unity."[19] This "sign" is expressed in that those who come to be brothers now include Protestants and Roman Catholics. Across the years Taizé's witness to Christian unity, whether at the base community in Burgundy or at the small communities (fraternities) scattered in disparate places throughout the world, has had three foci. They are: (1) common worship and prayer, (2) work for social justice and (3) ministry with youth.

Undoubtedly one of Taizé's lasting contributions to the ecumenical movement lies in its concept of corporate worship, expressed in the Taizé liturgy and in the community's particular prayers for unity. The Taizé liturgy, which might be used in North America, Chile, Italy, South India, Wales, or anywhere in the world, is a proclamation of the power and joy of the Resurrection. To sit or kneel in the Taizé chapel, the Church of Reconciliation, is to experience the unity given by God to a frightened and divided people. One senses in the community's worship the reason for Taizé's power.

Members' prayers for unity do not end in the sanctuary, but propel the community and those it touches into active work in the service of the ecumenical movement. Frère Eric tells the story of God's redeeming love through his stained glass windows; Frère Max is a widely published theologian and is currently a staff consultant to the World Council of Churches, helping to draft the historic consensus on Baptism, Eucharist, and Ministry, which will be in the spotlight at the Vancouver Assembly (1983); Frère Roger works tirelessly to unite Protestants and Roman Catholics by such means as courageous conversations with the Pope pressing for more visible signs of reconciliation.

For Taizé unity is found also in the search for social justice, or, as Frère Roger calls it, "the pastoral care of the masses."[20] A primary expression of this concern is found in their pattern of sending "fraternities" of two or three brothers to live and serve among the poor of the earth. The names of the cities—Tokyo, Seoul, Chittagong (Bangladesh), Algoinas (Brazil), New York and Nairobi—indicate their identification with people in places where destitution, poverty and alienation are the accepted lifestyle. The brothers of Taizé speak of the dynamic of Christian unity as "struggle and contemplation to become men and women of communion."[21] This means sharing life with the poorest of the poor and engaging sacrificially in the struggle for human rights.

In the early 1970s thousands of youth and students, inspired by Taizé's witness, began to invade the solitude of the community. Frère Roger believed this phenomenon arose from the alienation these youth felt because of a divided church and divided generations:

> Denominationalism evokes a negative reaction among the younger generations, who reject all reference to a history which no longer relates to the present. . . . If we do not offer them in the near future a Church United, which in our faith we confess as the only place for united brotherhood of all men, then they will search elsewhere and will turn to universalist ideologies or to a spiritual atheism.[22]

This surprise package of youth in search of faith began to change the ministry and, to some degree, the character of the Taizé community. Simply feeding and caring for such hordes of laughing, questing youth is a herculean task. While 2,500 people gather on some summer weekends, it is not uncommon during Holy Week for 10,000 young people from various countries to gather in the church and in tents for worship and Bible study, for dialogue and response to the issues of the contemporary human drama.

In order to coordinate and give momentum to this youth movement, a Council of Youth was announced in 1970; after careful preparations its first meeting was held at Taizé in 1974 with 40,000 participants. Ever since, teams of youth from all six continents gather from time to time with Frère Roger in some part of the world to draft a pastoral letter. In 1974 the *First Letter to the People of God* called upon Christians to be one united people, ready to be "a contemplative people, thirsting for God; a people of justice, living the struggle of the exploited; a people of communion, where the nonbeliever also finds a creative place." *A Second Letter to the People of God 1976*, written from Calcutta, affirmed, "The People of God can build up a parable of sharing in the human family." A third letter, *The Acts of the Council of Youth 1979*, was written from one of the poorest slums of Africa and was read in December 1978 to a European conference at Paris. Its message is a living motif at Taizé: the winter of the church has ended. A springtime has come whose sign of life makes it possible for us to participate in "creative communion" with the whole people of God and to widen our solidarity with all humanity. Through these youth, and through its fraternities, its liturgy and its witness, Taizé speaks and lives out an authentic ecumenism: visible unity in the midst of struggle and contemplation.

The Community of Grandchamp

A less well-known but equally vital community of ecumenism is that of the sisters of Grandchamp. Located near the Swiss village of Areuse some fifteen miles from Neuchâtel, this community of women dressed in pale blue habits radiates the spirit of unity that comes from a life of prayer. The history of the Grandchamp community in its beautiful Swiss Romande setting goes back to 1931. A group of women, mostly from the French-speaking part of the Reformed Church of Switzerland, were drawn together for silence, prayer and meditation; they came in search of a deep spiritual life in order that they might give a clear Christian witness. Among them was Madame Léopold Michéli, who later became Sister Geneviève, the community's first leader. Five years later a retreat house was officially opened and the large number of those who came gave evidence that a great need was being met. In 1952 a new community was formally constituted as a part of the ministry of prayer of the Reformed Church of Switzerland. From the early days sisters representing different Protestant traditions came from Switzerland, Germany, France, Holland and Spain. Upon joining the Grandchamp community they assumed the same calling: to live together a parable of unity and communion. One of their first decisions was to adopt the Rule of Taizé as guidance for their community and the Taizé liturgy for their worship, since it was recognized early in the planning that the purpose of the two communities was the same. This friendly relation between Grandchamp and Taizé allows members of both to pursue the same vocation in different ways. Grandchamp has a long tradition of spiritual retreats for laypeople.

Grandchamp is by charter and daily example a sign of reconciliation in the world Christ loves. It seeks to accomplish this witness by being a community at prayer, by welcoming people who come for spiritual renewal and by going into the world as a sign of the presence of Christ among the needy. At the center of life at Grandchamp is the chapel, l'Arche, where the sisters and others gather for prayer four times a day. When you hear that among the people they are known as ''the Upper Room of the Church,'' you get a sense of Grandchamp's ministry. Grandchamp is very much in the world, as are all communities of ecumenical spirituality.

Like Taizé, the Grandchamp community believes its vocation is to be both ''present to God'' in their prayer and worship, and ''present to the world'' in their welcome to those who come seeking peace and new life. As a sign of the presence of Christ in the world the sisters also have commissioned fraternities, small groups living out their faith in the areas of human distress, poverty and crisis. They are there to love and pray, to be a sign of hope for those who are ignored or rejected. The locations of these mini-communities change from time to time. Earlier they were found in the drab sections of Beirut, Lebanon and in the industrial outskirts of Paris. Today they are in Algeria, Israel, Nicaragua, France and different parts of Switzerland. In each case they become a sign of the spirit of Christian unity, dealing with the hurts of a wounded people and drawing together Christians of all traditions. In a society of brutal violence Grandchamp is determined to express "a violence of love" which brings faith in Christ to humanity.

The Ecumenical Institute Bossey

In view of Lake Geneva, a mile from the Swiss village of Céligny, stands the stately eighteenth-century Château de Bossey, surrounded by a cluster of more modern buildings. Here since 1946 the World Council of Churches has provided a unique center for ecumenical study and leadership development. Bossey was the dream of W.A. Visser 't Hooft, the first general secretary of the WCC, who realized that the ecumenical movement needs a place where the vision of ecumenism can be explored and experienced. Here the global Christian community has come and gone for conferences of all sorts, testifying to the pain of the world's brokenness and the hope of Christian unity.

The aims and functions of the Ecumenical Institute Bossey constitute a courageous and vitally essential ministry. Its purposes are:
  1. to provide training for future generations of ecumenical leaders, both clergy and lay;
  2. to promote ecumenical theology within the framework of intercultural and interconfessional encounters;
  3. to bring together in an ecumenical spirit the universal vocation of the church to unity and mission with the concrete demands of regional and local ecumenism;
  4. to create a community in which ecumenism is experienced and shared;
  5. to practice ecumenical education with wider perspectives in a broader context;
  6. to share in an ecumenical spirituality that respects the diversity of liturgical traditions.

Bossey's program includes four kinds of activities. (1) The Graduate School of Ecumenical Studies meets from mid-October to mid-February with approximately sixty participants from twenty-five to thirty countries. With all the diversity of God's created world, the students wrestle with the meaning of the Christian faith for our time through seminars, Bible study and community worship. They share their culture and music; they have "days of solidarity" with people in poor and oppressed countries; they exemplify the church in its brokenness; they become the church in its unity. Through these occasions the future leaders of the Church Universal are prepared for ecumenical ministry and service. (2) A series of courses for laypeople, pastors and church workers takes place in the spring and summer. Participants immerse themselves in one of a variety of themes, such as Orthodox spirituality, African religion and culture, the church's role in human development, the prospects of peace, the family crisis, the Bible in today's world, healing, death in different cultures, the shape of Christian unity. Each year's program deals with a fascinating group of ecumenical problems; a catalog of the issues addressed over the past thirty years would startle the mind. (3) At Bossey specialized consultations on problems and concerns of the ecumenical movement also take place. (4) It is the place where church groups and individuals come for orientation to the ecumenical movement. Increasingly, many are seeking to make it a place for spiritual rest and renewal.

The Ecumenical Institute Bossey is a place where the miracle of ecumenical education takes place in the hearts and minds of thousands of people, a community where church and world meet, sometimes in debate and conflict, ofttimes in reconciliation. It is a place where Christians constantly seek frontiers of witness and service in a world where the church is called to be a sign of hope, a place where church unity is unashamedly confessed amid the tragic disunity of Christians. At Bossey the essence of ecumenism takes shape as the wandering people of God create Christian community.

Ecumenical Summer Mission Conferences

A particularly North American expression of the spirit, the Ecumenical Summer Mission Conferences have evolved largely as a movement of lay Christians. Across the span of the twentieth century they have provided practical exposure and experience in ecumenism to several million persons. Their history is closely intertwined with that of the Missionary Education Movement, the National Council of Churches in the U.S.A. and the Canadian Council of Churches, and with the history of Friendship Press.

The movement had its origins in 1900 in a meeting between Silas H. Paine, owner of the Silver Bay Hotel on Lake George, New York, and Luther D. Wishard, a secretary of the International Committee of the Young Men's Christian Association.[23] At this meeting, Wishard asked Paine to consider using the hotel and its grounds as a gathering place for Christians "for the study of the Bible and missions." Wishard's main concern was to provide facilities for organizations interested in training young people for lives of Christian service. A man of both vision and action, he had already initiated mission study programs in the Presbyterian and Congregational churches when he discovered that more students were volunteering for overseas service than the churches were prepared to support.

The first summer conference at Silver Bay, held in 1901, was The Forward Movement Council of Bible Study and Foreign Missions of the Congregational Churches. At its conclusion, Wishard proposed a series of interdenominational conferences for the summer of 1902.

An important development during that summer was the formation of the Young People's Missionary Movement of the United States and Canada, through which fifteen denominational boards cooperated to promote missionary education in North America. According to Dr. T.H.P. Sailer, a leader who participated in the conferences, attendance rose from 300 in 1903 to 600 two years later.

The organization was renamed the Missionary Education Movement in 1911. Its leaders were largely responsible for raising money to build five cottages, which were among the first classrooms at Silver Bay. These memorial buildings were a tribute to five missionaries: Walter Macon Lourie, a Presbyterian; J. Addison Ingle, an Episcopalian; Adoniram Judson, a Baptist; Samuel J. Mills, a Congregationalist; and John G. Paton, a Scots Presbyterian.

The program of the Missionary Education Movement had three main points of focus: mission education in the church in its broadest sense; training for missionary leaders; and organization of mission work in the local church. Among the early leaders were Dr. John R. Mott, Harlan P. Beach, Samuel Zwemer, Sherwood Eddy, Robert E. Speer and Dr. Sailer, who summarized the significance of the movement:

> While it is difficult to be sure that any event is absolutely the first in its field it seems safe to say that the summer conferences of the YPMM were pioneers in the study of missions.... [They] gave birth to similar conferences in other parts of the country of which one at Asilomar is still in operation. ... The spirit of the conferences has sent many volunteers out to the home and foreign mission fields and has inspired more to promote and conduct missionary education in their local churches.

CHRISTIAN UNITY: MATRIX FOR MISSION

Today, Ecumenical Summer Mission Conferences are held across North America and are attended by laypersons from churches in the United States and Canada. In 1981, for example, the list included Eastern Ecumenical Conference on the Christian World Mission, Silver Bay; Minnesota School of Missions, St. Paul; Mission Education Conference, Sheboygan, Wisconsin; Mt. Sequoyah Ecumenical Conference, Fayetteville, Arkansas; Northern New England School of Religious Education, Geneva Point Center, New Hampshire; Northwest International Christian Mission Conference, Newberg, Oregon; Pacific Southwest Conference of World Christian Mission, Asilomar, California; Southeast Christian Mission Conference, Montreat, North Carolina.

The Southeast Christian Mission Conference is the latest addition, with a 1980 attendance of 400 adults, 100 youth and 50 children.

Each conference is essentially autonomous, freely choosing to focus on the interdenominational themes in education for mission. Attendance typically includes lay Protestants from the mainline denominations, with some representation from evangelical groups and increasing numbers of Roman Catholics. Many conferences provide programs for children and youth, as well as adults.

These four examples of ecumenical encounters are not presented as exclusive models, though many people who touch our lives have drawn inspiration from these sources. What they do give us are insights into the dynamics required for ecumenical spirituality and witness, which can take place anywhere — in congregations, lay groups, ministerial clusters or new ecumenical groups formed in response to this calling. How have these examples, and particularly the European communities, defined and developed the distinguishing marks of spiritual ecumenism? They present to us five points. (1) They are profoundly committed to Christian unity. Each deliberately attracts Christians of all shades and hues, and each understands its life as a sign of reconciliation to divided humanity. (2) They believe that spirituality — prayer, communion, Scripture study — is the dynamism of Christian unity. (3) They understand their community to be a place where the church and the world authentically meet. Mission is the expression of faith. (4) They see the need for repentance, beginning with themselves, as preparation for their calling to unity and mission. Smugness about disunity or indifference to the needs of the contemporary world are considered cardinal sins. (5) They are committed to a holiness of life, that is, to offer their lives to God to use as God wills. These are signs of a spirituality for ecumenism that can change the world.

7 The Shape of the Church to Come

Our present danger is not that of creating a "super church." It is rather the danger of accepting something less than the Church Christ gives us.

—**COCU Principles of Church Union, 1967**

Now that we have considered various aspects of our common calling to unity, and especially in the changing context in which this unity is pursued, we must turn at last to an exploration of the nature of Christian unity itself. If the churches are to advance toward unity, they must have a common vision of their goal. What kind of unity are we seeking? What sort of unity animates the journey—our prayers, our conferences, our mission involvements and our negotiations? This is a key question since the integrity of the ecumenical movement depends upon our seeing clearly what this unity is and how it can be lived out. All our labors will have little meaning unless we share a common goal.

If this is the crux of Christian unity, it is also the most difficult question. In the first fifty years of the ecumenical movement, the nature of unity was not fully explored. This is understandable when one listens to some of the incomplete definitions that circulated among the churches. One perspective focused on unity as a return to the "Mother church." Not long ago members of the Orthodox churches, the Roman Catholic Church (before Vatican Council II) or the Church of Christ could stop a conversation in mid-sentence with the assertion that they alone held and embodied God's truth. The way to unity, seen from this perspective, is the absorption of all other Christians into their tradition. A second negative image surfaces when Christian people think of unity as *merger,* placing people in an organizational unity without due regard for their differences or their spiritual convictions. Usually merger carries the unhappy vision of one tradition or cluster of traditions dominating and swallowing up the others. This, too, is a distortion of the nature of true unity.

A more subtle and at times unconscious image for unity assumes that *our* denomination is best and that the shape of Christian unity will be like *our* church, with a few adjustments in order to include the other churches. According to this view, unity is The United Methodist Church multiplied by five, or the Episcopal Church writ large, or whatever your church happens to be. These arguments overlook the fact that unity includes mutuality of gifts and graces from the different churches. They also assume that unity is only the continuation of what now exists; there is little awareness of the need of all Christians for deep renewal as a basis for visible unity.

Fortunately, the ecumenical movement believes that the shape of the unity God wills for and gives to the church—the unity that we must express—is far different from any of the above.

A SPIRITUAL AND VISIBLE SHAPE

To begin with, we should lay the cards on the table and end the age-old dichotomy between spirit and form in Christian unity. As we saw in an earlier chapter, the dynamic power of the search for Christian unity is spirituality, a life of prayer and meditation and of sharing together the bread of life. The deepest signs of our unity in Christ are spiritual. But spiritual unity cannot be interpreted simply as an invisible relationship that leaves unchanged the outward forms of the churches. Prominent ecumenist Albert C. Outler calls this an "ecumenism within the status quo" which leaves "the old order of visible divisions open and glaringly revealed before the eyes of the world."[1] Such a disembodied spiritual unity does little to overcome the estrangements among Christians in matters of faith, ministry, sacraments, missionary presence and social witness. To settle for a spiritual unity that does not sooner or later become a visible, tangible fellowship is unsatisfactory and unbiblical.

Genuine spirituality acknowledges that real unity in Christ, through the Holy Spirit, has to be incarnated in the church's forms, structures and institutions. Bishop Lesslie Newbigin has witnessed many times to the fact that spiritual unity among Christians is necessarily an incarnate, churchly unity: "Christianity is, in its very heart and essence, not a disembodied spirituality, but life in a visible fellowship, a life which makes such total claim upon us, and so engages our total powers, that nothing less than the closest and most binding association of men [and women] with one another can serve its purpose."[2]

In 1809 Thomas Campbell, one of the patriarchs of the Christian Church (Disciples of Christ), published his famous apologia for Christian unity, *Declaration and Address*. Its first proposition asserts that "The Church of Christ upon earth is essentially, intentionally and constitutionally one; consisting of all those in every place that profess their faith in Christ and obedience to Him in all things according to the Scriptures, and that manifest the same by their tempers and conduct."[3] Unity as *koinonia* (fellowship) is more than cordiality toward those who differ from us, more than a warm feeling of belonging to one family, to the one flock of Christ. As Lukas Vischer, former director of the Faith and Order Secretariat of the WCC, has put it, "Fellowship cannot be merely an idea. If it is to become effective it must assume form and structures."[4] Unity includes real, tangible relationships and structures that constitute our life together. Unity means that we share in the experiences of faith and mission in such dramatic ways that both we and the world can see and know that Christians are one. This sort of visible spiritual unity challenges the status quo and calls into question our old ways and loyalties and structures. Spirit and form go together in ecumenism as in all aspects of life. The church's unity must be manifested concretely and historically. That is the first principle to make clear about the nature of the unity ahead of us.

UNITY OF THE ROAD AND UNITY OF THE GOAL

What shape should this "visible spiritual unity" actually take? What models and patterns have we found to be effective steps for moving toward the unity we seek? And what is the content of that ultimate goal? In his book, *The Pressure of Our Common Calling*, which I believe is required reading for anyone who would grasp the ecumenical vision, W.A. Visser 't Hooft makes a helpful distinction between "the unity of the road" and "the unity of the goal."[5] By the "unity of the road," Dr. Visser 't Hooft means the unity of our provisional efforts, that measure of unity experienced in the multitude of approaches and activities that dot the ecumenical landscape. It is the unity that "holds us together right now and obliges us to go forward together." "The unity of the goal" is the ultimate fellowship we seek, the unity that "is promised to us and which will be given to us in God's time if we respond obediently to His work of gathering.'' One is the unity that presently exists, or could soon exist, in the midst of the churches; the other is the fuller unity that belongs to the Church of Christ and that the churches must manifest.

The value of this distinction is that it shows the relationship between the provisional models and the ultimate models of unity. Such a contrast, on the one hand, keeps us from accepting some interim unity as the only unity God requires. On the other hand, we are made aware of the interim steps and relationships that help make the fuller unity possible.

The following pages present three models of "unity on the road" that are actually used, at least to some extent, by churches in the ecumenical movement. As we survey these models, let us keep two points in mind. (1) These are not substitutes for the final goal we seek, but provisional patterns of church relationship. They are important, they express a certain degree of visible unity, but they remain only partial. (2) These models should not be thought of as sequential. *Cooperation*, for example, does not necessarily lead in a direct line to *covenant* or *organic* fellowship. Often these patterns overlap. For instance, a church born out of the organic union of previously separated churches may enter into forms of cooperation or covenant with other churches. The important thing is that they all be seen as movements toward the ultimate destination of full visible unity in Christ.

VISIBLE UNITY AS COOPERATION

Since the beginning of the twentieth century, the ecumenical movement has found its main structured expression in councils of churches. Their constituencies and styles may differ. At the international level is the World Council of Churches. At the regional level are such organizations as the All-Africa Council of Churches, the Christian Conference of Asia or the Latin America Council of Churches. National councils include the National Council of Churches of Christ in the U.S.A., the Canadian Council of Churches and the British Council of Churches. And there are state or metropolitan councils — the Indiana Council of Churches, the Texas Conference of Churches (a *conference* of churches in the United States often denotes Roman Catholic membership), the New York Metropolitan Council of Churches. Cooperation may also take the form of particular programs shared among several congregations, judicatories or women's groups. In each instance the churches agree to work together in common mission and service, while the autonomy of each church is preserved.

Like all models of unity on the road, cooperation has both strengths and weaknesses. For many years it was the primary approach favored by pragmatic, denominationally-minded North American Christians. In many instances it has been a way of preparing for and deepening a partial unity. In cooperation authority remains in the divided churches, but they are able to come out of their denominational isolation and work together in a wider spectrum of activities, ranging from Christian education to social and political questions. Through councils of churches, a heroic Christian voice has been impressively articulated on many public issues facing our world.

The limitation of cooperative action is that it is often considered an alternative to full unity rather than a way station "on the road." Churches can cooperate without being changed or reconciled. They can participate in certain programs and projects without their own lives being transformed. And churches can so define councils and conferences that they effectively guarantee the self-preservation of the divided churches.

The major criterion for evaluating any ecumenical model is whether it fosters the reconciliation of the churches involved. Councils are no different. Unless a council of churches keeps alive at its center the urgency of Christian unity, and unless it is constantly calling the churches to a wholeness cemented in covenant and sacramental life as well as in witness and service, it loses its reason for existence. How can we proclaim reconciliation to the world when we are not reconciled with one another? How can we be ambassadors of the one Lord when we cannot ourselves live together under the Lord's rule?

In this sense any council is an interim body pointing to a deeper life of reconciliation. As was once said about the WCC:

> Our council has therefore an interim character, marks a stage on the road, is a body living between the time of the complete isolation of the churches from each other and the time—on earth or in heaven—when it will be visibly true that there is one Shepherd and one flock.[6]

When such a commitment to unity becomes central to the life of a council, it knows its role is to be "a transitory phase of the journey from disunity to unity."[7] To become merely the defender of denominations is, in the final analysis, to become an antiecumenical body.

This call to a deeper unity can be heard in many places today. The Anglican Consultative Council states that "The co-operation of Christians is now in a phase which cries out for intercommunion."[8] The report of a commission of the National Council of Churches in the U.S.A., appointed to restate the purposes of that important ecumenical body, has offered an equally forceful judgment:

> The unity of the Church is more binding than cooperation allows, more vital than efficiency suggests. Christ holds us together still in "an everlasting covenant" with sacred bonds to him, to one another and to all creation. Unity in Christ leaves no room for any autonomy of tradition, culture, ethnicity, race, class, sex, politics (or anything else that we call "Christian pluralism") by which we justify our division.[9]

In summary, cooperation can be a valuable instrument of "unity on the road," but it is not our destination. It is a model of divided Christianity. As you read the following words of Lesslie Newbigin, think of the unity confessed by the churches in your town or city:

> The unity that Christ wills for us is something more than cooperation. It is a unity of being—the new being of the new man in Christ. It is the unity which is described in St. John's Gospel as abiding in him and he in us. It is the unity which comes from entering into the perfect at-one-ment which he has wrought for us in the Cross. Our divisions are a public contradiction of that atonement. Cooperation in common programs of study and action is not a substitute for this unity.[10]

Cooperation can be seductive. It does not require repentance. The churches can become content with peaceful coexistence as the best or the only model of ecumenism available. But peaceful coexistence is far from being true reconciliation. Coexistence is simply a more respectable expression of disunity.

VISIBLE UNITY AS COVENANTAL FELLOWSHIP

The covenant offers a valuable expression of unity on the way. Both the Old and New Testaments present the covenant as a means by which humans are bound to God and one another. God said to Noah, Abraham, Moses and Jeremiah, "I will be your God and you shall be my people," and a group of diverse nomadic tribes became a single cohesive community. The covenant defined and gave form to their identity. Through these covenants the relationship between God and the people deepened and Israel found her purpose in human history.

Christians have believed that a renewal of these covenants came in Jesus Christ. He is the "new covenant." In him God again sealed the promises of justice and hope. He became Emmanuel, God with us. Moreover, this new covenant called into being a community of faith, the church, through which all those who believe in his name are made one.

The key insight to be drawn at this point is that God's covenant binds together Christian people across their natural differences and their warring ways, creating community, fellowship and unity among them. Without exaggeration we can say that our present disunity is a violation of our covenant with God.

Listen to Frederick W. Dillistone, an Oxford scholar whose book, *The Structure of the Divine Society,* teaches with timely words:

> The very word covenant suggests a coming-together, the bridging of a chasm, the transcending of a dualism, the creating of an intimate union. It is implied that two parties have been standing over against one another in separation and uncertainty, and that now a new relationship is being established which will bring them together in a union of a permanent character.[11]

Dillistone is, of course, referring to the everlasting pledge between God and the people of God. But this divinely initiated covenant also calls for a new relationship between ourselves and others. We are supposed to live in "covenantal bonds" with all those who confess the name of Christ, and to reach out for those as yet outside the covenant. We are bound together with friends and enemies, insiders and outsiders in a community of surprising and wonderful variety.

What does the covenantal model imply about the shape of our unity? (1) Covenanting shifts the focus away from our human actions and concentrates instead on what God has done and is doing and on what we should do in response. (2) Covenantal unity does not allow patterns of domination or the subordination of one partner to another. The covenant affirms relations and forms of the church that are nonhierarchical, decentralized, and that invite the participation of the whole people. (3) The visible shape of unity or union is discovered through an emphasis upon relationships rather than structures. In such an approach, structures emerge from trust in one another and from a new awareness of one another's gifts and graces. (4) The pattern of the covenant commits the partners to use their resources within a single relationship. Shared resources — people, money, spirituality—and shared decision making are earnest signs of a shared life.

In Wales and England we have two solid illustrations of what this kind of unity on the way can mean.[12] According to plans set forth in both places, covenanting for unity involves the following: acknowledgment of one another as full Christian churches; mutual recognition of one another's members and the eventual preparation of joint rites of baptism and confirmation; invitation of one another's members to the Lord's Supper "without question"; acceptance of one another's ordained ministries as "true ministries of Word and sacrament in the holy catholic church"; development of joint decision making in order to act together in witness and service.[13] Covenantal unity is a pledged togetherness. The churches offer one another reconciliation, even though the final shape of unity is not yet known. Whether the Welsh and English churches will find the faith and courage to covenant is a decision still to come. Nevertheless, the model they set forth may prove valuable in other settings where churches seek to express a visible unity "on the road."

VISIBLE UNITY AS ORGANIC UNION

Those who use the phrase *organic union* to describe the nature of Christian unity have experienced rough waters lately. Some even question whether the phrase can survive as a working term. Yet, between 1925 and 1980, nearly 70 united churches were formed out of the organic union of two or more previously separated churches. Presently, 34 negotiations of organic union involving 120 churches from all continents remain faithful to this vision of unity in a changing world. But resistance to this organic image, an image found in the apostle Paul's theology, is clearly in evidence.

Organic union involves living together in a common structure, yet the past two decades have witnessed a growing distrust of structures. People acknowledge that many structures in society and in the church have lost their meaning. A common assumption holds that most structures dominate the individual and stifle freedom and spontaneity. What must be understood, however, is that organic unity is not a political or business merger; it need not lead to monolithic organizations that impose a uniformity of liturgy and faith. Those who use *uniformity* as a synonym for *organic union* betray either a biased theology or a failure to recognize the authentic unity-in-diversity of united and uniting churches around the world.

We need to remember that the term organic union is not a description of an organization. It refers to a decision by independent and diverse Christians to form a common structure and to work for the enrichment of that new body. ''An organism is a unity, where each member is an instrument in the general plan, where each member has its appointed purpose or function, where each member can only act, and be understood, and indeed exist, through the end and aim of the whole.''[14] This quotation is directed toward Greek political theory, but it is applicable also to our understanding of the church and its unity. In an organically united church, every member's ultimate loyalty is to the whole body and not to just one part of it. The sacraments are sacraments of the whole body. The ministry is accepted by the previously separate traditions as a ministry of the whole body. Paul's image of the body and its members, particularly in 1 Corinthians 12:14-26, gives us the clue. The foot, the hand, the eye and the ear are essential, individual members with different functions, but their highest significance is in their working relationship in the one body. This is not structural uniformity but a rich and vital interaction of diverse but complementary parts.

The organic dimension of unity presses us to view the ecumenical task in several significant ways. (1) It is a model of unity ''on the road'' in which every single member (and every local congregation) is viewed as an essential part of the whole church. Unity ceases to be an abstract idea and becomes a local reality. (2) In organic unity diversity is at once included and reconciled in the church's life, but this diversity functions for the sake of the whole. Consequently the organically united church is understood as the arena for the maximum interplay of tradition with tradition. Such organically united churches as the United Church of Canada (a union of Congregationalists, Methodists and Presbyterians), the Church of South India (Anglicans, Methodists, Presbyterians and Congregationalists) and the United Church of Christ in the United States (Congregational and Evangelical and Reformed) demonstrate this interplay. (3) Organically united churches aim at reaching out more effectively in service and mission because of the common structure. This, too, is borne out by the actual experience of united churches around the world. (4) Finally, most united churches understand themselves to be a *uniting* as well as a united church. This is why we speak of organic union as ''on the road.'' The shape of unity attained at a particular place and at a particular moment of history, however celebrated the united church may be, is understood to be incomplete and provisional in character. Nationally or regionally, united churches must certainly press for a visible unity that is wider in membership and perspective. ''The separate churches desire not merely to form a new and larger denomination, but to embark on a pilgrimage whose ultimate goal can be the unity of the whole Body.''[15]

These three models of unity on the road—cooperation, covenant, organic union—must not be seen as alternatives, since each presents important insights about church unity. As F.W. Dillistone points out, ''Through the constant interplay of the organic and the covenantal principles there comes into existence a growing 'togetherness' as well as a developing freedom, a unity in diversity, a fulfillment of the individual within the framework of the corporate whole.''[16]

THE UNITY OF THE GOAL: THREE DESCRIPTIONS

Having looked at these images of unity on the road, we must now tackle the formidable task of describing some elements of the final unity we seek. What is the vision that calls us forward? Three models of the ''unity of the goal'' have been projected by the churches themselves, and each deserves careful consideration. Once again, however, we will find that these are not so much alternative models as different, tentative expressions of a shared vision.

1. The first image comes from the Third Assembly of the WCC at New Delhi (1961), which presented a classic description of the shape of Christian unity. It is an attempt to express more clearly ''the nature of our common goal ... the vision of the one Church [which] has become the inspiration of our ecumenical endeavour.'' The New Delhi statement is one of the longest but most crucial sentences ever written in the ecumenical movement. Maybe we can grasp better its meaning in outline:

We believe that the unity which is both God's will and his gift to his Church

is being made visible as
all in each place
who are baptized into Jesus Christ and confess him
as Lord and Savior
   are brought by the Holy Spirit into one fully
      committed fellowship,
   holding the one apostolic faith,
   preaching the one Gospel
   breaking the one bread,
   joining in common prayer,
   and having a corporate life reaching out in
      witness and service to all

and who at the same time are united with the whole
Christian fellowship in all places and all ages

in such wise that ministry and members are accepted by all,
and that all can act and speak together as occasion requires
for the tasks to which God calls his people.[17]

This surely is unity in the flesh! The various parts of this seminal statement deserve closer attention.

The primary focus of this portrait is that unity is made visible "in each place" and "in all places and ages." In other words, unity is both local and universal. The word "place" means primarily a local neighborhood, but given the changing situation of human relationships, it also includes other settings in which Christians need to express their visible unity in Christ — schools, offices, factories. "Place" may apply also to wider geographical areas—cities, states or nations—and certainly refers to all kinds of Christian people in each "place" regardless of race and class.

The phrase "fully committed fellowship" points to the character and intensity of this unity. Fellowship (*koinonia*) cannot depend merely on an institution or organization; "a lively variety marks corporate life in the one Body of the Spirit."[18] But it does portray an intimacy of life among churches that is far more than living side by side, either in competition or amicable isolation. To be "fully committed" means to be united to Christ and to one another. The symbols of such a "fully committed fellowship" are nothing less than proclaiming the one apostolic faith, participating in common praise and prayer, acknowledging a common baptism, regularly sharing in a common eucharist, and joining in the one mission of Christ in the world through "a corporate life reaching out." That phrase, "a corporate life reaching out," says a great deal about the unity of the church. It says that visible unity is imperative for the fulfillment of our missionary responsibilities. As we engage in mission, "the vision of one Church proclaiming one Gospel to the whole world becomes more vivid and the experience and expression of our given unity more real."[19]

Church unity, in addition to being local, is also universal, global, catholic. This element was reinforced at the next WCC Assembly at Uppsala, Sweden (1968), which described visible unity as "a dynamic catholicity," a universal community where people of different churches, cultures and races are brought into "an organic and living unity in Christ!" Two symbols of this unity "in all places and ages," according to the member churches of the WCC, are (1) the mutual acceptance of the members and ministries of each church by all, and (2) the ability of the churches to "act and speak together." Both these signs of the future, however, constitute unresolved difficulties in the present. Not all the churches as yet accept one another's ministries as valid; nor have they been able to establish a forum or council through which they can teach the faith and engage in witness and service together. These are primary targets for the future of ecumenism.

Although no church has acted officially on the New Delhi statement, it does give essential guidance for our consideration of the shape of church unity. The amazing, and often unknown, fact is that between the New Delhi (1961) and Uppsala (1968) assemblies over twenty united churches were constituted, most containing the elements of unity set forth in this description of the ecumenical goal. If this becomes the future shape of the church, the distinctive witness of the denominations will be renewed and reconciled into a diverse but organic pattern of life and witness.

2. A second description of the church's unity was produced in 1973—at a WCC consultation in Salamanca, Spain, on "Concepts of Unity and Models of Union"—and affirmed two years later at the Nairobi Assembly. This is the vision of one church as a "conciliar fellowship." Our consideration requires that we quote the full text:

> The one Church is to be envisioned as a conciliar fellowship of local churches which are themselves truly united. In this conciliar fellowship, each local church possesses, in communion with the others, the fullness of catholicity, witnesses to the same apostolic faith, and therefore recognizes the others as belonging to the same Church of Christ and guided by the same Spirit. As the New Delhi Assembly pointed out, they are bound together because they have received the same baptism and share the same Eucharist; they recognize each other's members and ministries. They are one in their common commitment to confess the gospel of Christ by proclamation and service to the world. To this end each church aims at maintaining sustained and sustaining relationships with her sister churches, expressed in conciliar gatherings whenever required for the fulfillment of her common calling.[20]

The similarities between the Nairobi and New Delhi descriptions are evident. Those who see them as alternative models of the unity "of the goal" have misunderstood both, since Nairobi merely elaborates on the message of New Delhi. The same elements of unity are present in both: expressing the apostolic faith, participating in one baptism and Eucharist, acknowledging the same ministry, confessing Christ to the world together through witness and service, having common structures of consultation and decision making. These elements give substance to what it means to be "truly united."

Beyond these elements, however, conciliar fellowship says something distinctive about the nature of this ecumenical life. First, each church would put an end to prejudices and historical animosities and would recognize the other churches "as belonging to the same Church of Christ and guided by the same Spirit." They are not strangers or competitors, but members of the same catholic community. They are local churches within the one Universal Church. Second, a new quality of fellowship is implied. Conciliar fellowship is marked by a sharing in the many diverse spiritualities and ways of worship, by a respect for diversities of culture, ethnicity and language, by a commitment to support one another in suffering and joy. The fruition of this unity would be a genuinely universal council that could represent the common witness of all the churches.

3. The third and most recent description of the goal speaks of our unity as "a communion of communions." It is the model proposed by the Roman Catholic Church, and seconded by some Episcopalians. The idea was put forth publicly in an address given during the Week of Prayer for Christian Unity in 1970 at Great St. Mary's Church, Cambridge, England, by Jan Cardinal Willebrands, the president of the Vatican Secretariat for Promoting Christian Unity.[21] Earlier, in an article in the British ecumenical journal *One in Christ,* Dom Emmanuel Lanne, O.S.B., a French ecumenist, proposed that the unity we seek is "a variety of typologies within the same ecclesial allegiance."[22] Building on this description, Cardinal Willebrands proposed as the model of visible unity the concept of "types" (from the Greek *typoi*), communions or "sister churches." The unity of the church, he said, can best be expressed in "a plurality of types" within the communion of the one and only Church of Christ.

Like all our descriptions of unity, this one needs some explaining. Each type or sister church has its own traditions of theology, liturgy, spirituality and discipline. There is a Roman Catholic *typos,* an Orthodox *typos,* a Moravian *typos,* a Baptist *typos* and so on. These would remain basically unchanged, but under the Willebrands proposal they would recognize one another as belonging to the one Church of Christ and live in "communion" with one another. The signs of this belonging would undoubtedly be common teaching on matters of faith and morals, Eucharist sharing and a common agreement on ministry and the papacy.

CHRISTIAN UNITY: MATRIX FOR MISSION

This is an intriguing model, especially since it shows a sensitivity to the existence of different Christian traditions. A full explanation of this model demands, however, an understanding of the complex word *communion*. For Roman Catholics, communion is a strong word. It is never used to describe relations of mere cooperation or any other ties that constitute less than a fully committed fellowship. If each tradition (*typos*) did not undergo significant change and share in the enrichments of the wider fellowship, a communion of communions would be little more than a federation of divided churches. If, however, the sister churches moved beyond their own separate identities into a common identity, if the gifts and vitalities of each church (or communion) were made part of the whole company of Christ's people, then the "communion of these communions" would be genuine.

Since Cardinal Willebrands's address, several ecumenical dialogues have chosen to highlight this model of unity. In a final report on *The Unity We Seek,* the Roman Catholic-Presbyterian dialogue in the United States concluded: "Our mutual conviction is that the shape of unity conceived in terms of a communion of communions is a very fruitful approach to future unity."[23] Further, in a consultation to evaluate its past ecumenical involvements and to set goals for the future, the Episcopal Church reached consensus on this concept, and gave concrete indications of what it might entail:

> The visible unity we seek will be one eucharistic fellowship. As an expression of and a means toward this goal, the uniting Church will recognize itself as a communion of Communions, based upon acknowledgment of catholicity and apostolicity. In this organic relationship all will recognize each other's members and ministries. All will share the bread and the cup of the Lord. All will acknowledge each other as belonging to the Body of Christ at all places and at all times. All will proclaim the Gospel to the world with one mind and purpose. All will serve the needs of humankind with mutual trust and dedication. And for these ends all will plan and decide together in assemblies constituted by authorized representatives whenever and wherever there is need.[24]

The interesting part of this description of the unity of the goal is not only the Episcopal adoption of "a communion of Communions," but the strong echoes it contains of conciliar fellowship as described by the WCC at Nairobi.

The three models described in this section are not so much alternative pictures of unity as different sketches of the same vision. The lines seem to be converging on a conciliar fellowship that visibly and organically expresses both the diversity and oneness of our life as the body of Christ.

VISIBLE UNITY AS CONCILIAR FELLOWSHIP

Many questions, of course, remain unanswered about such a conciliar fellowship, whatever its ultimate form. But several observations can be made even at this point in our search for a truly and visibly united church.

1. Conciliar fellowship must go hand in hand with organic unity. Some seem to think that conciliar fellowship can be expressed through current denominational structures. According to this understanding, the churches would fully recognize one another and would meet from time to time in a universal council, but they would also continue their separate existences and the development of their own traditions of worship, theology and spirituality. True conciliar fellowship, however, at least as it has been envisioned at Nairobi and in many subsequent meetings, involves *truly united* local churches. "Conciliar fellowship,' said the delegates at Nairobi, "does *not* look toward a conception different from that full organic unity sketched in the New Delhi statement, but a further elaboration of it. The term is intended to describe an aspect of the life of the one undivided church at all levels."[25] The Salamanca conference delivered the same warning.

2. The phrase "truly united" indicates a unity that is a dynamic movement. Unity is never a static, already-achieved relation. God's world is active, in process of becoming, and God's people are constantly responding to a growing life. This dynamic movement presses the churches beyond the differences and tensions that now divide them. It gives them a flexibility to face the conflicts that arise as the church witnesses to the gospel in a divided world. A truly united local church sees its life as a sign and instrument of the divine purpose to draw divided cultures and peoples into God's one family.

3. Conciliar fellowship points to a quality of life among the churches. This qualitative unity is revealed by the full mutual recognition of congregations who accept and welcome one another, by the common celebration of the Eucharist, by a common striving to understand and express the faith delivered to the church, by a sense of the rich interdependence among congregations, by the commitment to decide together about the fulfillment of their missionary tasks in each place.

CHRISTIAN UNITY: MATRIX FOR MISSION

4. The vision of conciliar fellowship shows us the need to manifest church unity at different levels—local, national, regional and universal. These are not different kinds of unity. We are speaking of the same reality whether in a small town, a metropolis, a nation or the world. At each level, in appropriate and visible ways, the risen Christ gathers the believers to send them into the world as the sign and foretaste of the Kingdom of God. The same marks of wholeness are present at all levels.

5. Finally, conciliar fellowship as a vision of unity indicates by its very title the need for a genuine universal council. "Council" in this context does not mean the councils of divided churches already in existence, such as the Seattle Council of Churches, the National Council of Churches and the World Council of Churches. These, as we have seen, are only interim instruments for the promotion of unity and common witness on the way. A genuine ecumenical council would be an expression of the one Christian community spread across the face of the earth. Representatives of the different parts of the church would gather regularly to confer and to decide together about major issues of truth, unity and mission. The council would not be merely a business assembly, but rather an expression of the communion among the once-divided churches.

What matters in the final analysis is whether we and the churches have the faith to follow this vision and to engage in a *costly unity*. We can never be one without surrendering to some extent the pride of our separate identities. True conciliar fellowship is a recognizable foretaste of the new humanity. It is the leaven of liberation and reconciliation. But we cannot be a leaven of reconciliation to humanity without paying the price of witness against those powers that oppress, deform and otherwise deny the humanity of millions of God's people. To this end, the search for unity takes us again and again to the cross of Christ. Pastors, laypeople, denominational executives—all discover that through suffering love we are truly able to understand what God wants of the church; to incarnate God's forgiveness to those caught in sin and alienation; to live in the assurance of victory through the Resurrection; to be inheritors of the Kingdom. Through the cross we can discern and accept the shape of Christian unity, which demonstrates God's reconciling love to the world. When churches are ready "to die with Christ," they will discover that the God who raised Jesus from the dead is able to renew and empower them through the Holy Spirit.

110

NOTES

Quotations from Vatican II documents are taken from Walter M. Abbott, S.J., general editor, *The Documents of Vatican II* (New York: Herder and Herder and Association Press, 1966).

Chapter 1: Unity, Diversity and Division

1. See Geiko Müller-Fahrenholz, ed., *Unity in Today's World:* Faith and Order Paper No. 88 (Geneva: World Council of Churches, 1978), pp. 82-85.
2. Ibid., p. 83.
3. W.A. Visser 't Hooft, ed., *The Evanston Report* (New York: Harper and Row, 1955), p. 87. The italics are mine.
4. Ibid., p. 87.
5. In his *Epistles to the Ephesians*, Homily XI, 5; quoted in Barry Till, *The Churches Search for Unity* (New York: Penguin Books, 1972), p. 78.
6. Yves Congar, O.P., *Ecumenism and the Future of the Church* (Chicago: Priory Press, 1967), p. 4.
7. James E. Wagner, "The Compulsions of a Church Unionist," in Robert McAfee Brown and David H. Scott, eds., *The Challenge to Reunion* (New York: McGraw-Hill, 1963), p. 19.
8. *Consultation on Church Union 1967: Principles of Church Union* (Cincinnati: Forward Movement Publications, 1967), p. 13.
9. See Sidney L. Mead, "Denominationalism: The Shape of Protestantism in America," in his *The Lively Experiment* (New York: Harper and Row, 1963), pp. 103-133.
10. Ibid., pp. 103, 104.
11. L.J. Trinterud, "The Task of the American Church Historian," *Church History* XXV (March, 1956), p. 9.
12. Winthrop Hudson, "Denominationalism as a Basis for Ecumenicity: A Seventeenth Century Concept," *Church History* XXIV (1955), pp. 32-50.
13. W.E. Garrison, *The Quest and Character of a United Church* (New York and Nashville; Abingdon Press, 1957), pp. 167-193.
14. Karl H. Hertz, "American Denominationalism: A Form of Indigenization," unpublished paper read at Ecumenical Institute Bossey, Céligny, Switzerland, July 1980.
15. Quoted in Hudson, "Denominationalism...."
16. See Ronald E. Osborn's important "The Role of the Denomination: An Essay in Ecclesiology," *Encounter* 22, no. 2 (Spring, 1961), pp. 160-179.
17. H. Richard Niebuhr, *The Social Sources of Denominationalism* (New York: Henry Holt, 1929), p. 6.
18. C.C. Morrison, *The Unfinished Reformation* (New York: Harper, 1953), pp. 28-47. Dr. Morrison's propositions included one which carried anti-Roman Catholic overtones, which he would not include if he were writing them today.
19. Ibid., pp. 48-57.

20. Roy I. Sano, "Ecumenical Commitment: A Fragile Gift," an unpublished address given to the National Association of Ecumenical Staff, Estes Park, Colorado, July 7, 1980.
21. See J.E. Lesslie Newbigin, "What is a Church Truly United?" in *In Each Place* (Geneva: World Council of Churches, 1977).
22. Dean R. Hoge, *Division in the Protestant House* (Philadelphia: Westminster Press, 1976), p. 74ff. Here he is following the analysis of Martin Marty, *Righteous Empire,* and David Moberg, *The Great Reversal.*
23. Ibid., p. 119.
24. Ibid., p. 122.
25. Ibid., p. 133.

Chapter 2: Is There a Crisis in Christian Unity?

1. Samuel McCrea Cavert, "Is the Ecumenical Movement Slowing Down?" *The Christian Century* (May 1, 1974), p. 476.
2. W.A. Visser 't Hooft in editorial, *The Student World* XXX, no. 2 (1937), p. 108.
3. L.A. Zander, "The Essence of the Oecumenical Movement," *The Student World* XXX, no. 2 (1937), pp. 161-162.
4. Michael Hurley, S.J., *Theology of Ecumenism* (Cork, Ireland: The Mercier Press, 1969), p. 10.
5. For the definitive work on the meaning and usage of "ecumenical," see W.A. Visser 't Hooft, *The Meaning of Ecumenical* (London: SCM Press, 1953) and his "The Word 'Ecumenical'—Its History and Use," in Ruth Rouse and S.C. Neill, eds., *History of the Ecumenical Movement, 1517-1948* (Philadelphia: Westminster Press, 1954), pp. 735-740.
6. Visser 't Hooft, *Meaning of Ecumenical,* p. 25.
7. J.H. Oldham, ed., *The Churches Survey Their Task;* Report of the Oxford Conference on Church, Community, and State (London: George Allen and Unwin, 1937), p. 168.
8. Oliver S. Tomkins, *The Church in the Purpose of God* (London: SCM Press, 1950), p. 8.
9. John A. Mackay, "Ecumenical: the Word and the Concept," *Theology Today* IX, no. 1 (April, 1952), p. 5.
10. World Council of Churches, *Minutes and Reports of the Fourth Meeting of the Central Committee, Rolle (Switzerland), August 4-11, 1951,* pp. 65, 66. The italics are mine.
11. "Towards Unity in Tension," *Uniting in Hope*; Faith and Order Paper No. 72 (Geneva: World Council of Churches, 1975), p. 90.

Chapter 3: Unity: The Biblical Perspective

1. James D. Smart, *The Strange Silence of the Bible in the Church* (Philadelphia: Westminster, 1970), pp. 15-16.
2. For this section I am indebted to Douglas Jones, *Instrument of Peace: Biblical Principles of Christian Unity* (London: Hodder and Stoughton, 1965).
3. J. Blauw, "The Mission of the People of God," in Charles C. West and David M. Paton, eds., *The Missionary Church in East and West* (London: SCM Press, 1954), p. 44.

4. C.H. Dodd, "The Church in the New Testament," in Albert Peel, ed., *Essays Congregational and Catholic* (London: Independent Press, 1931), p. 15.
5. See Ernst Käsemann, "Unity and Multiplicity in the New Testament Doctrine of the Church," in his *New Testament Questions of Today* (London: SCM Press, 1969), pp. 253-259; and James D.G. Dunn, *Unity and Diversity in the New Testament* (Philadelphia: Westminster Press, 1977).
6. See E.F. Scott, *The Varieties of New Testament Religion* (New York: Charles Scribner's Sons, 1944).
7. See Helmut Koester, "Gnomai Diaphori; The Origin and Nature of Diversification in the History of Early Christianity," in James M. Robinson and Helmut Koester, *Trajectories Through Earliest Christianity* (Philadelphia: Fortress Press, 1971), pp. 120-121.
8. Robert McAfee Brown, *The Ecumenical Revolution,* rev. ed. (Garden City: Anchor-Image Books/Doubleday, 1969), p. 9.
9. Käsemann, "Unity and Multiplicity...," p. 257.
10. Paul S. Minear, *Images of the Church in the New Testament* (Philadelphia: Westminster Press, 1969).
11. See William R. Baird, "The Nature of the Unity of the Church in the New Testament," *The College of the Bible Quarterly* XXXIV, no. 4 (October, 1957), p. 2.
12. Paul S. Minear, *Jesus and His People* (London: Lutterworth Press, 1956), pp. 55, 56.
13. Claude Chavasse, *The Bride of Christ* (London: Faber and Faber, 1939), p. 17.
14. See Lionel S. Thornton, *The Common Life in the Body of Christ* (London: Dacre Press, 1942).
15. See Markus Barth, *Ephesians: 4-6, The Anchor Bible* (Garden City: Doubleday, 1974), p. 461.
16. W.A. Visser 't Hooft, *The Pressure of Our Common Calling* (Garden City: Doubleday, 1959), p. 85.
17. Barth, *Ephesians,* p. 497.
18. Paul S. Minear, "Evangelism, Ecumenism, and John Seventeen," *Theology Today* 35, no. 2 (April, 1978), p. 5.
19. See Raymond E. Brown, *The Gospel According to John (XIII-XXI), The Anchor Bible* (Garden City: Doubleday, 1970), pp. 769 ff.
20. W.A. Visser 't Hooft, *Pressure of...Calling,* p. 81.
21. Ibid., p. 83.

Chapter 4: Unity and Mission: The Heretical Dichotomy

1. Arthur J. Brown, *Unity and Missions* (New York: Fleming H. Revell, 1915).
2. V.S. Azariah in H.N. Bate, ed., *Faith and Order: Proceedings of the World Conference, Lausanne, August 3-21, 1927* (London: SCM Press, 1927), p. 10.
3. *Consultation on Church Union 1967; Principles of Church Union* (Cincinnati: Forward Movement Publications, 1967), pp. 11-12.
4. Norman Goodall, ed., *Missions Under the Cross* (London: Edinburgh House Press, 1953), p. 193. The italics are mine.
5. William Barclay, *More New Testament Words* (London: SCM Press, 1958), p. 102.

6. Peter Berger, "A Call for Authority in the Christian Community," in Paul A. Crow, Jr., ed., *Digest of the Proceedings of the 10th Meeting of the Consultation on Church Union, Denver, September 27-30, 1971,* vol. X, p. 126.

7. Quoted by Hans J. Margull, "Presence and Proclamation," reprinted in Donald McGavran, ed., *Eye of the Storm; the Great Debate in Mission* (Waco, Texas: Word Books, 1972), p. 227.

8. Johannes C. Hoekendijk, *The Church Inside Out* (Philadelphia: Westminster Press, 1966), p. 23. This idea was first presented by the great missionary theologian Martin Kähler.

9. René Voillaume, *Seeds of the Desert — The Legacy of Charles de Foucauld* (Chicago: Fides Publishers, 1955), p. vii. The italics are mine.

10. Ibid., p. 17.

11. *The Christian Community in the Academic World* (Geneva: World Student Christian Federation, 1964), p. 8. See *The Student World* LVII, no. 4 (1964), pp. 357-368.

12. Ronald K. Orchard, *Missions in a Time of Testing* (London: Lutterworth Press, 1964), p. 93.

13. Max Warren, *Challenge and Response; Six Studies in Missionary Opportunity* (New York: Morehouse-Barlow Co., 1959), p. 74.

14. Burgess Carr, in a statement at the Nairobi Assembly of the World Council of Churches, 1975.

15. See Harold E. Fey, *Cooperation in Compassion: The Story of Church World Service* (New York: Friendship Press, 1966).

16. W.A. Visser 't Hooft, in a statement to the Provisional Committee of the World Council of Churches, 1946.

17. Robert C. Mackie, quoted in Fey, *Cooperation in Compassion,* p. 206.

18. *Who Cares? Service 1969* (Geneva: CICARWS, 1969), p. 13.

19. *The New Delhi Report; The Third Assembly of the WCC, 1969* (London: SCM Press, 1962), pp. 111, 93.

20. Nikos A. Nissiotis, "The Ecclesiological Significance of Inter-Church Diakonia," *The Ecumenical Review* XIII, no. 2 (January, 1961), p. 193.

21. Minutes of the Commission on Inter-church Aid, Refugee and World Service, Strasbourg, France, 1978.

22. *La Vie Protestante,* August 4, 1966, pp. 3, 5; quoted in Jacques Rossel, *Mission in a Dynamic Society* (London: SCM Press, 1968), p. 85, footnote.

23. Emilio Castro, *Amidst Revolution* (Belfast: Christian Journals Ltd., 1975), pp. 61-62.

24. J.G. Davies, *Worship and Mission* (London: SCM Press, 1966), p. 102.

25. Patrick C. Rodger and Lukas Vischer, eds., *The Fourth World Conference in Faith and Order; Montreal 1963* (London: SCM Press, 1964), p. 78.

Chapter 5: The Unity of the Church and the Reconciliation of the Human Family

1. José Miguez-Bonino, "A Latin American Attempt to Locate the Question of Unity," *The Ecumenical Review* XXVI, no. 2 (April, 1974), pp. 210-223.

2. Ibid., p. 54.

3. Ibid., p. 60.

4. Ibid.

· 5. *Your Kingdom Come; Report on the World Conference in Mission and Evangelism, Melbourne, Australia, 12-25 May 1980* (Geneva: World Council of Churches, 1980), p. 180.

6. "The Gospel of Justice: Monseñor Among His People," *Christianity and Crisis* 40, no. 8 (May 12, 1980), p. 127. This address was taped and translated for publications by Jorge Lara-Braud, a close friend of the archbishop, and Claudia Rosenhouse.

7. See Roger Schutz, *The Power of the Provisional* (London: Hodder and Stoughton, 1969), pp. 30-40.

8. *Churches Responding to Racism in the 1980s;* report of the WCC World Consultation on Racism, Noordwijkerhout, Netherlands, June 16-21, 1980 (*PCR Information* No. 9), p. 5.

9. Ibid., p. 40.

10. *In Quest of the Church of Christ Uniting; An Emerging Theological Consensus,* revised 1980 (Princeton, N.J.: Consultation on Church Union, 1970), p. 51.

11. *A Plan of Union for the Church of Christ Uniting* (Princeton: Consultation on Church Union, 1970), p. 22.

12. Ibid., p. 28.

13. *In Quest of the Church of Christ,* p. 53.

14. Ibid.

15. David M. Paton, ed., *Breaking Barriers, Nairobi 1975* (Grand Rapids: Wm.B. Eerdmans, 1976), p. 62.

16. "The Unity of the Church and the Handicapped in Society," in Choan-Seng Song, ed., *Growing Together in Unity* (Madras: Christian Literature Society and the World Council of Churches, 1978), p. 124.

17. *In Quest of the Church of Christ,* p. 56.

18. Ibid.

19. See Constance F. Parvey, ed., *Ordination of Women in Ecumenical Perspective;* Faith and Order Paper No. 105 (Geneva: World Council of Churches, 1980), p. 37. This is the report on a WCC Consultation at Klingenthal, Austria, 1979. See the excellent bibliography of literature on the ordination of women, pp. 75-94.

20. "What Unity Requires," in *Breaking Barriers, Nairobi 1975,* p. 62.

Chapter 6: Spirituality and Ecumenism

1. See O.U. Kalu, *Divided People of God; Church Union Movement in Nigeria: 1875-1966* (New York and Lagos: NOK Publishers, 1978), pp. 66-78.

2. Roger Schutz, *The Power of the Provisional* (London: Hodder and Stoughton, 1969), p. 47.

3. G.K.A. Bell, "A Sermon," *The Ecumenical Review* XI, no. 1 (October, 1958), p. 7.

4. Maurice Villain, *Unity; A History and Some Reflections,* 3rd rev. ed. (London: Harvill Press, 1963), pp. 196-197.

5. Urban T. Holmes, *A History of Christian Spirituality* (New York: Seabury Press, 1980), p. 2.

6. *The Evanston Report; The Second Assembly of the World Council of Churches 1954* (London: SCM Press, 1955), p. 91.

7. Villain, *Unity,* p. 193.

8. Foreword to Thomas Merton, *Contemplative Prayer* (Garden City: Doubleday/Image Books, 1969), p. 14.

9. Ruth Rouse and S.C. Neill, eds., *History of the Ecumenical Movement, 1517-1948* (Philadelphia: Westminster Press, 1954), p. 345.
10. Gregory Baum, *That They May Be One* (London: Bloomsbury Publishing Co.), p. 130.
11. Quoted in John J. Higgins, S.J., *Thomas Merton On Prayer* (New York: Doubleday, 1973), p. 14.
12. Ibid.
13. Thomas Merton, *Contemplative Prayer* (Garden City: Doubleday/Image Books, 1971), p. 41
14. Henri J.M. Nouwen, *Clowning in Rome; Reflections on Solitude, Celibacy, Prayer, and Contemplation* (Garden City: Doubleday/Image Books, 1979), p. 72.
15. Schutz, *Power of the Provisional*, p. 76.
16. Quoted in Villain's chapter in *Paul Couturier; apôtre de l'unité chrétienne* (Lyon, France; Imprimerie Emmuel Witte, 1954), pp. 19-42.
17. Villain, *Unity; A History and Some Reflections*, p. 218.
18. *The Rule of Taizé* (Taizé: Les Presses de Taizé, 1968), p. 21.
19. Schutz, *Power of the Provisional*, p. 60.
20. Ibid., p. 25.
21. See Roger Schutz, *Struggle and Contemplation* (London: SPCK, 1973).
22. Schutz, *Power of the Provisional*, pp. 17, 18.
23. Material on the history of Silver Bay and the founding of the Missionary Education Movement is taken from E. Clark Worman, *The Silver Bay Story* (Silver Bay, N.Y.: Silver Bay Association, 1952). Direct quotes are from p. 19 (Luther Wishard) and from pp. 28-29 (Dr. Sailer).

Chapter 7: The Shape of the Church to Come

1. Albert C. Outler, *That the World May Believe* (New York: Board of Missions of the Methodist Church, 1966), p. 43.
2. J.E. Lesslie Newbigin, *The Household of God* (New York: Friendship Press, 1954), pp. 76-77.
3. Thomas Campbell, *Declaration and Address* (Washington, Pa.: Brown and Sample, 1809), prop. 1.
4. Reinhard Groscurth, ed., *What Unity Implies* (Geneva: World Council of Churches, 1969), pp. 75-76.
5. W.A. Visser 't Hooft, *The Pressure of Our Common Calling* (Garden City: Doubleday, 1959), p. 21.
6. *The Church;* Faith and Order Paper No. 7 (London: SCM Press, 1951), p. 52.
7. Newbigin, *Household of God*, p.13.
8. Anglican Consultative Council, *Partners in Mission; Report of the Second Meeting, Dublin, Ireland, 1973* (London: SPCK, 1973), p. 2.
9. National Council of Churches, *Foundations for Ecumenical Commitment* (New York: National Council of Churches, 1980), p. 19.
10. Lesslie Newbigin, *One Body, One Gospel, One World* (London and New York: International Missionary Council, 1958), p. 54.
11. F.W. Dillistone, *The Structure of the Divine Society* (London: Lutterworth Press, 1951), p. 33.

12. See Paul A. Crow, Jr., "Covenanting as an Ecumenical Paradigm," *Mid-Stream* XIX, no. 2 (April, 1980). This essay was also published with others by Robert S. Paul et al., in a special COCU issue of the *Austin Seminary Bulletin* XCVI (March, 1981).

13. See *Towards Visible Unity: Proposals for a Covenant* (London: Churches' Council for Covenanting, 1980).

14. Ernest Barker, *The Political Thought of Plato and Aristotle,* quoted in Dillistone, *Structure of Divine Society,* p. 21.

15. *Consultation on Church Union 1967; Principles of Church Union* (Cincinnati: Forward Movement Publications, 1967), p. 26. See also Gerald F. Moede, *Oneness in Christ: The Quest and the Questions* (Princeton: COCU, 1981).

16. Dillistone, *Structure of Divine Society,* p. 222.

17. W.A. Visser 't Hooft, ed., *The New Delhi Report* (London: SCM Press, 1962), p. 116.

18. Ibid., p. 120.

19. Ibid., p. 121.

20. David M. Paton, ed., *Breaking Barriers; Nairobi 1975* (Grand Rapids: Wm. B. Eerdmans, 1976), p. 60. See Salamanca report in *What Kind of Unity?* Faith and Order Paper No. 69 (Geneva: World Council of Churches, 1974), p. 121.

21. See Jan Cardinal Willebrands, "Moving Toward a Typology of Churches," *Catholic Mind* 68 (April, 1970), pp. 35-42.

22. Emmanuel Lanne, "Pluralism and Unity," *One in Christ* V, no. 3 (1970), pp. 430-451.

23. Ernest L. Unterkoefler and Andrew Harsanyi, eds., *The Unity We Seek; A Statement by the Roman Catholic/Presbyterian-Reformed Consultation* (New York: Paulist Press, 1979), p. 15.

24. "Ecumenical Affairs—Declaration on Unity," *Journal of the General Convention of the Protestant Episcopal Church in the United States of America* (September, 1979), p. C-46.

25. *Breaking Barriers, Nairobi, 1975,* p. 60.

INDEX

Merton, Thomas, 81, 82
Methodists, 56, 68
Miguez-Bonino, Jose, 62
Minear, Paul S., 34
Mission
  and unity, 27, 43ff
  as presence, 49
  as proclamation, 46ff
  worldwide, 26
Missionary Education Movement, 93
Mission and Evangelism World Conference,
  63
Mission Conferences, North American, 92
Mission/Evangelism as Eucharist, 57ff
  as service, 52ff
Morrison, Charles Clayton, 15
Mugabe, Robert, 51
Muslims, 28, 49

National Council of the Churches of Christ,
  92, 100
Newbigin, Lesslie, 16, 96, 100
Niebuhr, H. Richard, 14, 15
Nigeria, 77
Nouwen, Henri, 81, 82

Oikoumene, 25, 38
Old Testament and unity, 30ff
Orthodox churches, 23, 74, 80
Orchard, Ronald K., 50
Organic unity, 102ff
Outler, Albert C., 96
Oxford Conference, Life and Work, 26

Paine, Silas H., 92
Paul, Apostle, 9, 33, 102-3
Paul VI, Pope, 55
Pentecost, 38
Pluralism, 20
Polarization, 17
  between sexes, 73
Poverty and unity, 65ff
Prayer
  and unity, 79ff
  Week of, see Week of Prayer
Presbyterians, 12, 49, 56
Presence and mission, 49ff
Proclamation, 46ff
Program to Combat Racism, WCC, 51

Racism, 67
  Program to Combat, 51
Reconciliation, 30
  and Unity, 60ff
Reformed churches, 12, 90
Reformers, 12
Rehabilitation and relief, 53
Resistance to unity
  historical, 22
  psychological, 21
  sociological, 22
  theological, 22
Road, unity of, 97ff
Roman Catholics, 12, 74, 79, 84, 88, 94,
  107
Romero, Oscar Arnulfo, 64, 66
Rouse, Ruth, 80

Sailer, T.H.P., 93

Sano, Roy I., 16
Schutz, Brother Roger, 66, 77, 81, 87, see
  also Taize
Sexism, 73ff
Shalom, 38
Söderblom, Nathan, 25
South Africa, 67
South India, Church of, 55, 103
Spirituality and unity, 77ff
Steere, Douglas V., 80

Taize Community, 66, 80, 86ff., see also
  Schutz, Brother Roger
Tensions of unity, 21, 28
Third World, 44
Todd, Garfield, 52
Tomkins, Oliver, 26

United Church of Canada, 103
United Church of Christ, 103

Vatican II decrees, 26, 34, 45, 79
Villain, Maurice, 79
Vischer, Lukas, 97
Visible unity, 26, 96ff.
  as conciliar fellowship, 109
  as cooperation, 98
  as covenantal fellowship, 100ff
  as organic unity, 102
Visser 't Hooft, W.A., 23, 28, 55, 91, 97

Warren, Max, 50
Wattson, Lewis Thomas, 84
Week of Prayer for Christian Unity, 84ff,
  107
White, Lurana, 84
Willebrands, Jan Cardinal, 107, 108
Wishard, Luther D., 93
Women
  and men, 73
  ordination of, 74
World Council of Churches, 63, 78, 99
  Assemblies: Evanston, 9, 54;
    Nairobi, 19, 27; New Delhi, 104;
    Uppsala, 27, 54, 105
  Central Committee, 27
  Consultation in Salamanca, 106
  Commission on Evangelism, 50
  Commission on Faith and Order, 27
  Commission on Inter-Church aid,
    Refugee and World
    Service, 53, 56
  prayer, 79
  Program to Combat Racism, 51
World Student Christian Federation, 50

Zimbabwe/Rhodesia, 51

119